BUS STOP

BY WILLIAM INGE

D0059229

DRAMATISTS
PLAY SERVICE
INC.

BUS STOP

BY WILLIAM INGE

★

DRAMATISTS
PLAY SERVICE
INC.

DRAMATISTS PLAY SERVICE, INC.

ESTABLISHED BY MEMBERS OF THE

DRAMATISTS GUILD
OF THE AUTHORS LEAGUE OF AMERICA

for the

HANDLING OF THE ACTING RIGHTS OF MEMBERS' PLAYS

and

THE ENCOURAGEMENT OF THE AMERICAN THEATRE

440 Park Avenue South, New York, NY 10016
www.dramatists.com

BUS STOP was first presented by Robert Whitehead and Roger L. Stevens at The Music Box, New York City, March 2, 1955. It was directed by Harold Clurman, and the set was designed by Boris Aronson. The cast was as follows:

ELMA DUCKWORTH, *a waitress* ....Phyllis Love
GRACE HOYLARD, *owner of the restaurant* ....Elaine Stritch
WILL MASTERS, *a Sheriff* ....Lou Polan
CHERIE, *a chanteuse* ....Kim Stanley
DR. GERALD LYMAN, *a former college professor* ....Anthony Ross
CARL, *a bus driver* ....Patrick McVey
VIRGIL BLESSING, *a ranch hand* ....Crahan Denton
BO DECKER, *a young rancher and cowboy* ....Albert Salmi

SCENES
The action of the play takes place in a street-corner restaurant in a small town about thirty miles west of Kansas City.

ACT I
A night in early March. 1:00 A. M.

ACT II
A few minutes later.

ACT III
Early morning. About 5:00 A. M.

BUS STOP

ACT I

The entire play is set inside a street-corner restaurant in a small Kansas town about thirty miles west of Kansas City. The restaurant serves also as an occasional rest stop for the bus lines in the area. It is a dingy establishment with few modern improvements: scenic calendars and pretty-girl posters decorate the soiled walls, and illumination comes from two badly shaded light bulbs that hang on dangling cords from the ceiling, there are several quartet tables with chairs, for dining, at far L. is the counter with six stools before it, running the depth of the setting, behind the counter are the usual restaurant equipment and paraphernalia (coffee percolator, dishes, glasses, hot plate, sink, electric refrigerator, etc.); on top of the counter are several large plates of doughnuts, sweet rolls, etc., under glass covers. Three sugar bowls and a few dishes. At the far R., close to the outside entrance-door, are a magazine stand and a rack of shelves piled with paper-back novels and books. At back C. is an old-fashioned Franklin stove. At the back R. is a great window that provides a view of the local scenery. Against the rear wall, beneath the window, are two long benches meant for waiting passengers. At the back L. is the rear door, close to the upper end of the counter. Above this door is a dim hand-painted sign, "Rest Rooms in the Rear." U. S. in the L. wall is the door to Grace's apartment. A closet below that door.

It is one A. M. on a night in early March and a near blizzard is raging outside. Through the window we can see the sweeping wind and flying snow. Inside, by comparison, the scene is warm and cozy, the Franklin stove radiating all the heat of which it is capable. Two young women. in uniforms that have lost their starched fresh-

*ness, are employed behind the counter. Elma is a big-eyed
girl still in high school. Grace is a more seasoned character in her thirties or early forties. A bus is expected
soon and they are checking, somewhat lackadaisically, the
supplies. Outside, the powerful, reckless wind comes and
goes, blasting against everything in its path, seeming to
shake the very foundation of the little restaurant building,
then subsiding, leaving a period of uncertain stillness.
When the curtain goes up, Elma stands far R., looking
out the large plate-glass window, awed by the fury of the
elements. Grace is at the telephone, an old-fashioned
wall phone behind counter U. L.*

Beat 1.1

ELMA. (U. R., *drying a glass.*) Listen to that wind. March is
coming in like a lion. (*Grace jiggles the receiver on the telephone
with no results.*) Grace, you should come over here and look out,
to see the way the wind is blowing things all over town.

GRACE. Now I wonder why I can't get th' operator.

ELMA. I bet the bus'll be late.

GRACE. (*Finally hanging up.*) I bet it won't. The roads are O.K.
as far as here. It's *ahead* they're havin' trouble. I can't even get the
operator. She must have more calls than she can handle. (*Crosses
D. L. behind counter, clears dishes from D. S. end of counter.*)

ELMA. (*Still looking out the window.*) I bet the bus doesn't *have*
many passengers.

GRACE. Prob'ly not. But we gotta stay open even if there's only
one. (*Takes dishes to sink.*)

ELMA. I shouldn't think anyone would take a trip tonight unless
he absolutely *had* to.

GRACE. Are your folks gonna worry, Elma?

ELMA. No—Daddy said, before I left home, he bet this'd happen.

GRACE. Well, you better come back here and help me. The bus'll
be here any minute and we gotta have things ready.

ELMA. (*Leaving the window, following Grace.*) Nights like this,
I'm glad I have a home to go to.

GRACE. (*Washing and drying.*) Well, I got a home to go to, but

1.1A

there ain't anyone in it.

ELMA. (*Puts tops on three sugar bowls on counter.*) Where's
your husband now, Grace?

GRACE. How should I know?

ELMA. (*Crosses R. with two sugars.*) Don't you miss him?

6

GRACE. No!.

ELMA. (*Puts sugars on tables.*) If he came walking in now, wouldn't you be glad to see him?

GRACE. You ask more questions.

ELMA. I'm just curious about things, Grace.

GRACE. Well, kids your age *are*. I don't know. I'd be happy to see him, I guess, if I knew he wasn't gonna stay very long.

ELMA. (*Crosses back to* u. s. *end of counter.*) Don't you get lonesome, Grace, when you're not working down here?

GRACE. Sure I do. If I didn't have this restaurant to keep me busy, I'd prob'ly go nuts. Sometimes, at night, after I empty the garbage and lock the doors and turn out the lights, I get kind of a sick feelin', 'cause I sure don't look forward to walkin' up those stairs and lettin' myself into an empty apartment.

ELMA. Gee, if you feel that way, why don't you write your husband and tell him to come back?

GRACE. (*Thinks a moment, leans on* D. S. *end of counter.*) 'Cause I got just as lonesome when he was here. He wasn't much company, 'cept when we were makin' love. But makin' love is *one* thing, and bein' lonesome is another. The resta the time, me and Barton was usually fightin'.

ELMA. (u. *of* Grace.) I guess my folks get along pretty well. I mean . . . they really seem to like each other.

GRACE. Oh, I know *all* married people aren't like Barton and I. Not all! (*Goes to* u. L. *telephone again. Elma goes to sink, dries glasses which she puts* D. S. *on counter.*) Now, maybe I can get the operator. (*Jiggles receiver.*) Quiet as a tomb. (*Hangs up.*)

ELMA. I *like* working here with you, Grace.

GRACE. Do you, honey? I'm glad, 'cause I sure don't know what I'd do without ya. Week ends especially.

ELMA. You know, I dreaded the job at first.

GRACE. (*Kidding her.*) Why? Thought you wouldn't have time for all your boy friends? (*Elma looks a little sour. Grace gets rag from sink, wipes counter.*) Maybe you'd have more boy friends if you didn't make such good grades. Boys feel kind of embarrassed if they feel a girl is smarter than they are.

ELMA. What should I do? Flunk my courses?

GRACE. (*Puts rag on sink.*) I should say not. You're a good kid and ya got good sense. I wish someone coulda reasoned with *me* when I was your age. But I was a headstrong brat, had to have my own way. I had my own way all right, and here I am now, a grass

7

widow runnin' a restaurant, and I'll prob'ly die in this little town and they'll bury me out by the backhouse. *(Will, the sheriff, comes in the front door, wind and snow flying through the door with him. He is a huge, saturnine man, well over six feet, who has a thick black beard and a scar on his forehead. He wears a battered black hat, clumsy overshoes, and a heavy mackinaw. He looks somewhat forbidding.)*

WILL. *(On entering.)* You girls been able to use your phone?

GRACE. No, Will. The operator don't answer.

WILL. That means all the lines are down. 'Bout time fer the Topeka bus, ain't it?

GRACE. Due now.

WILL. You're gonna have to hold 'em here, don't know how long. The highway's blocked 'tween here and Topeka. May be all night gettin' it cleared.

GRACE. I was afraid a that.

WILL. They got the highway gang workin' on it now and the telephone company's tryin' to get the lines back up. March is comin' in like a lion, all right.

GRACE. Yah.

WILL. *(Taking off his mackinaw, hanging it, going to the fire to warm his hands.)* The station house's cold. Got any fresh coffee?

GRACE. *(Goes to coffee urn.)* It just went through, Will. Fresh as ya could want it.

WILL. *(Goes to counter.)* A storm like this makes me mad. *(Grace laughs at his remark and gives him a cup of coffee.)* It does. It makes me mad. It's just like all the elements had lost their reason.

GRACE. *(Stands behind counter near Will.)* Nothin' you can do about a wind like that.

WILL. Maybe it's just 'cause I'm a sheriff, but I like to see things in order.

GRACE. Let the wind blow! I just pray to God to leave a roof over my head. That's about all a person can do. *(The sound of the bus is heard outside, its great motor coming to a stop.)*

WILL. Here it is.

GRACE. Better fill some water glasses, Elma. *(Elma gets water pitcher, fills glasses.)* Remember, the doughnuts are left over from yesterday but it'll be all right to serve 'em. We got everything for sandwiches but cheese. We got no cheese.

8

WILL. You *never* got cheese, Grace. (*Rises, crosses* R.)

GRACE. (U. S. *of counter.*) I guess I'm kinda self-centered, Will. I don't care for cheese m'self, so I never think t' order it for someone else.

ELMA. Gee, I'm glad I'm not traveling on the bus tonight.

GRACE. I wonder who's drivin' tonight. This is Carl's night, isn't it?

ELMA. I think so.

GRACE. Yes it is. (*Obviously the idea of Carl pleases her. She nudges Elma confidentially.*) Remember, honey, *I* always serve Carl.

ELMA. Sure, Grace. (*The front door swings open, some of the snow flying inside, and Cherie, a young blonde girl of about twenty, enters as though driven. She wears no hat, and her hair, despite one brilliant bobby pin, blows wild about her face. She is pretty in a fragile, girlish way. She runs immediately to the counter to solicit the attention of Grace and Elma. She lugs along an enormous straw suitcase that is worn and battered. Her clothes, considering her situation, are absurd: a skimpy jacket of tarnished metal cloth edged with not luxuriant fur, a dress of sequins and net, and gilded sandals that expose brightly enameled toes. Also, her make-up has been applied under the influence of having seen too many movies. Her lipstick creates a voluptuous pair of lips that aren't her own, and her eyebrows also form a somewhat arbitrary line. But despite all these defects, her prettiness still is apparent, and she has the appeal of a tender little bird. Her origin is the Ozarks and her speech is Southern.*)

CHERIE. (*Anxious, direct.*) Is there some place I kin hide?

GRACE. (*Taken aback.*) What?

CHERIE. There's a *man* on that bus . . . I wanta *hide.*

GRACE. (*Stumped.*) Well, gee . . . I dunno.

CHERIE. (*Seeing the sign above the rear door* U. L., *starting for it.*) I'll hide in the powder room. If a tall, lanky cowboy comes in here, you kin just tell him I disappeared.

GRACE. (*Her voice stopping Cherie at the door.*) Hey, you can't hide out there. It's cold. You'll freeze your . . .

CHERIE. (*Having opened the door, seeing it is an outside toilet.*) Oh! It's outside.

GRACE. This is just a country town.

9

CHERIE. (*Starting again.*) I kin stand anything fer twenty minutes.

GRACE. (*Stopping her again.*) I got news for ya. The bus may be here all night.

CHERIE. (*Turning.*) What?

GRACE. The highway's blocked. You're gonna have to stay here till it's cleared.

CHERIE. (*Shutting the door, coming to counter, lugging her suitcase. She is about to cry.*) Criminey! What am I gonna do?

GRACE. (*Comes from behind counter, gets coat and goes to front door.*) I better go out and tell Carl 'bout the delay. (*Goes out front door.*)

CHERIE. (*Dropping to a stool at the counter.*) What am I gonna do? What am I ever gonna do?

ELMA. (*In a friendly way.*) There's a little hotel down the street.

CHERIE. What ya take me for? A millionaire?

WILL. (*Coming to Cherie with a professional interest.*) What's the trouble, Miss?

CHERIE. (*Looking at Will suspiciously.*) You a p'liceman? (*Rises, a step* L.)

WILL. I'm the local sheriff.

ELMA. (C. *behind counter. Feeling some endorsement is called for.*) But everyone likes him. Really!

CHERIE. Well . . . I ain't askin' t' have no one arrested.

WILL. Who says I'm gonna arrest anyone? What's your trouble?

CHERIE. I . . . I need protection.

WILL. What from?

CHERIE. There's a man after me. He's a cowboy.

WILL. (*Looking around.*) Where is he?

CHERIE. He's on the bus asleep, him and his buddy. I jumped off the bus the very second it stopped, to make my getaway. But there ain't no place to *get* away to. And he'll be in here purty soon. You just *gotta* make him lemme alone.

WILL. Ya meet him on the bus?

CHERIE. No. I met him in Kansas City. I work at the Blue Dragon night club there, down by the stockyards. He come there with the annual rodeo, and him and the resta the cowboys was at the night club ev'ry night. Ev'ry night there was a big fight. The boss says he ain't gonna let the cowboys in when they come back next year.

WILL. (C.) Then he followed ya on the bus?

10

CHERIE. He *put* me on the bus. I'm bein' abducted.

WILL. Abducted! But you took time to pack a suitcase!

CHERIE. I was goin' somewhere else, tryin' to get away from him, but he picked me up and carried me to the bus and put me on it. I din have nothin' to say about it at all.

WILL. Where's he plan on takin' ya?

CHERIE. Says he's got a ranch up in Montana. He says we're gonna git married soon as we get there.

WILL. And yor against it?

CHERIE. I don't wanta go up to some God-forsaken ranch in Montana.

WILL. Well, if this cowboy's really takin' ya against yor will, I s'pose I'll have to stop him from it.

CHERIE. You just don't know this cowboy. He's mean.

WILL. I reckon I kin handle him. You relax now. I'll be around mosta the night. If there's any trouble, I'll put a stop to it.

ELMA. You're safe with Will here. Will is very respected around here. He's never lost a fight.

WILL. What're ya talkin' about, Elma? Of course I've lost a fight . . . once.

ELMA. Grace always said you were *invincible*.

WILL. There ain't no one that's . . . *invincible*. A man's gotta learn that, the sooner the better. A good fighter has gotta know what it is to *get* licked. Thass what makes the diff'rence 'tween a fighter and a *bully*. (*Goes* U. R., *gets magazine from rack and sits on bench by window.*)

CHERIE. (*Shuddering.*) There's gonna be trouble. I kin feel it in my bones. (*Enter Dr. Gerald Lyman, a man of medium height,* about fifty, with a ruddy, boyish face that smilingly defies the facts of his rather scholarly glasses and iron-gray hair. He wears an old tweed suit of good quality underneath a worn Burberry. His clothes are mussed, and he wears no hat, probably having left it somewhere, for he has been drinking and is, at present, very jubilant. He looks over the restaurant approvingly.*)

DR. LYMAN. Ah! "This castle hath a pleasant seat."

CHERIE. (D. L. *end of counter. To Elma.*) Could I hide my suitcase behind the counter, so's he won't see it when he comes in? I ain't gonna say anything to him at all 'bout not goin' on to Montana with him. I'm just gonna let 'im think I'm goin' 'til the bus pulls out and he finds I ain't on it. Thaas th' only thing I know t' do. (*Crosses to stove.*)

ELMA. (*Taking the suitcase and putting it behind counter,* U. R. *end.*) Oh, you needn't worry with Will here.

CHERIE. Think so? (*She studies Will.*) Looks kinda like Moses, don't he? (*Crosses to counter, sits on stool* D. L.)

ELMA. He *is* a very religious man. Would you believe it? He's a deacon in the Congregational Church.

CHERIE. (*Just because she happens to think of it.*) My folks was Holy Rollers. Will ya gimme a cup of coffee, please? Lotsa cream. (*Elma draws a cup of coffee for her. Then Carl, the bus driver, comes in, followed by Grace. Carl is a hefty man, loud and hearty, who looks very natty in his uniform.*)

WILL. (*Calling to him from across the room.*) Howdy, Carl! You bring this wind? (*Cherie drinks her coffee.*)

CARL. (*Hollering back.*) No! It brought me! (*This greeting probably has passed between them a dozen times, but they still relish it as new.*)

GRACE. (*Slaps Carl on shoulder.*) Aren't you the comedian? (*Takes off coat, puts it in closet and crosses to counter.*)

CARL. The wind is doin' ninety miles an hour. The bus is doin' twenty. What's your guess about the roads, Will?

WILL. (*Rises, moves* C.) They got the highway gang out. It may take a few hours.

CARL. Telephone lines down, too?

WILL. Yah. But they're workin' on 'em. (*Dr. Lyman, having got his extremities warmed at the fire, seeks Carl privately to make certain clarifications.*)

DR. LYMAN. Driver, it seems to me we are still in the state of Kansas. Is that right?

CARL. What do ya mean, still? You been in the state of Kansas about a half hour.

DR. LYMAN. But I don't understand. I was told, when I left Kansas City, that I would be across the state line immediately. And now I find . . .

CARL. (*Eying Dr. Lyman suspiciously.*) You was kinda anxious to get across that state line, too, wasn't you, Jack?

DR. LYMAN. (*Startled.*) Why . . . what ever do you mean?

CARL. Nothin'. Anyway, you're across the line now. In case you didn't know it, Kansas City is in *Missouri.*

DR. LYMAN. Are you joking?

CARL. There's a Kansas City, Kansas, too, but *you* got on in Kansas City, Missouri. That's the trouble with you Easterners. You don't know anything about any of the country west of the Hudson River.

DR. LYMAN. Come, come now. Don't scold.

GRACE. (*As Carl gets out of his heavy coat.*) Carl, let me hang up your coat fer ya, while you get warm at the stove. (*She bangs up his coat as he moves to stove. Dr. Lyman's eyes brighten when he sees Elma, and he bows before her like a cavalier.*)

DR. LYMAN. "Nymph in thy orisons, be all my sins remembered!" (*Moves D. L. to counter.*)

ELMA. (*Smiling.*) I'm sorry your bus is held up.

DR. LYMAN. Oohh! Is that a nice way to greet me?

ELMA. (*Confused.*) I mean . . . (*Grace is U. C. near Carl L. of stove.*)

DR. LYMAN. After my loving greeting, all you can think of to say is, "I'm sorry your bus is held up." (*Sits on stool at counter.*) Well, I'm not. I would much rather sit here looking into the innocent blue of your eyes than continue riding on that monotonous bus. (*Grace gets coffee, takes it to Carl.*)

ELMA. Don't you have to get somewhere? (*Will gets magazine, drifts to bench by window.*)

DR. LYMAN. I have a ticket in my pocket to Denver, but I don't have to get there. I never have to get *anywhere*. I travel around from one town to another just to prove to myself that I'm *free*.

ELMA. The bus probably won't get into Denver for another day.

DR. LYMAN. Ah, well! What is our next stop?

ELMA. Topeka.

DR. LYMAN. Topeka? Oh, yes! that's where the famous hospital is, isn't it?

ELMA. The Menninger Clinic? Yes, it's a very famous place. Lots of movie stars go there for nervous breakdowns and things.

DR. LYMAN. (*Wryly.*) Does the town offer anything else in the way of diversion?

ELMA. It's the capital of Kansas. It's almost as big as Kansas City. They have a university and a museum, and sometimes symphony concerts and plays. I go over there every Sunday to visit my married sister.

13

DR. LYMAN. Aren't there any Indian tribes around here that have war dances?

ELMA. (*Laughing.*) No, silly! We're very civilized.

DR. LYMAN. I'll make my own judgment about that. Meanwhile, you may fix me a double shot of rye whiskey . . . on the rocks. (*Rises, moves* R.)

ELMA. (*Leans on counter.*) I'm sorry, sir. We don't sell drinks.

DR. LYMAN. You don't sell drinks?

ELMA. Not intoxicating drinks. No, sir.

DR. LYMAN. Alas!

ELMA. We have fresh coffee, homemade pies and cakes, all kinds of sandwiches . . .

DR. LYMAN. No, my girl. You're not going to sober me up with your dainties. I am prepared for such emergencies. (*Draws a pint bottle of whiskey from his overcoat pocket.*) You may give me a bottle of your finest lemon soda. (*Elma gets bottle of lemon soda from refrigerator.*)

ELMA. (*Whispering.*) You'd better not let Will see you do that. You're not supposed to.

DR. LYMAN. Who is *he*, the sheriff?

ELMA. Yes. Lots of people do spike their drinks here and we never say anything, but Will would have to make you stop if *he* saw you.

DR. LYMAN. I shall be *most* cautious. I promise. (*She sets the bottle of soda before him as he smiles at her benignly. He pours some soda in a glass, then some whiskey, and ambles over to a table, far* R., *sitting down with his drink before him. Will rises, moves over to Carl, who's at the end of the counter chiding Grace, where the two of them have been standing, talking in very personal voices that can't be overheard.*)

WILL. I sure don't envy ya, Carl, drivin' in weather like this. (*Grace crosses behind counter.*)

CARL. (*Making it sound like a personal observation.*) Yah! March is comin' in like a *lion.*

WILL. This all the passengers ya got?

CARL. There's a coupla crazy cowboys rolled up in the back seat, asleep. I thought I woke 'em, but I guess I didn't.

WILL Shouldn't you go out and do it now?

CARL. I'd jest as soon they stayed where they're at. One of 'em's a real troublemaker. You know the kind, first time off a ranch and

14

wild as a bronco. He's been on the make fer this li'l blonde down here . . . (*Indicates Cherie.*)

WILL. She was tellin' me.

CARL. I've had a good mind to put him off the bus, the way he's been actin'. I say, there's a time and place for ev'rything.

WILL. That bus may get snowbound purty soon.

CARL. I'll go wake 'em in a minute, Will. Just lemme have a li'l time here. (*Will sizes up the situation as Carl returns his attention to Grace, then Will picks up a copy of the Kansas City Star, sitting down close to the fire to read. Carl leans over counter.*) Ya know what, Grace? This is the first time you and I ever had more'n twenty minutes t'gether.

GRACE. (*Coyly.*) So what?

CARL. Oh, I dunno. I'll prob'ly be here mosta the night. It'd sure be nice to have a nice li'l apartment to go to, some place to sit and listen to the radio, with a good lookin' woman . . . somethin' like you . . . to talk with . . . maybe have a few beers.

GRACE. That wouldn't be a hint or anything, would it?

CARL. (*Faking innocence.*) Why? Do you have an apartment like that, Grace?

GRACE. Yes, I do. But I never told *you* about it. Did that ornery Dobson fella tell you I had an apartment over the restaurant?

CARL. (*In a query.*) Dobson? Dobson? I can't seem to remember anyone named Dobson. (*Elma is washing, drying dishes behind counter.*)

GRACE. You know him better'n *I* do. He comes through twice a week with the Southwest Bus. He told me you and him meet in Topeka sometimes and paint the town.

CARL. Dobson? Oh, yah, I know Dobson. Vern Dobson. A prince of a fella.

GRACE. Well, if he's been gabbin' to you about my apartment, I can tell ya he's oney been up there *once*, when he come in here with his hand cut, and I took him up there to bandage it. Now that's the oney time he was ever up there. On my word of honor.

CARL. Oh, Vern Dobson speaks very highly of you, Grace. Very highly.

GRACE. Well . . . he better. Now, what ya gonna have?

CARL. (*Sits on stool at counter.*) Make it a ham and cheese on rye.

GRACE. I'm sorry, Carl. We got no cheese.

15

CARL. What happened? Did the mice get it?

GRACE. None of your wise remarks.

CARL. O.K. Make it a ham on rye, then.

GRACE. (*At breadbox.*) I'm sorry, Carl, but we got no rye, either.

DR. LYMAN. (*Chiming in, from his table.*) I can vouch for that, sir. I just asked for rye, myself, and was refused. (*Elma, at stove, watches.*)

CARL. (*Turns.*) Look, Mister, don't ya think ya oughta lay off that stuff till ya get home and meet the missus?

DR. LYMAN. The *missus*, did you say? (*He laughs.*) I have no missus, sir. I'm *free*. I can travel the universe, with no one to await my arrival anywhere.

CARL. (*Sits on stool at counter. To Grace, bidding for a little sympathy.*) That's all I ever get on my bus, drunks and hoodlums. (*Dr. Lyman signals Elma for more soda.*)

GRACE. How's fer whole wheat, Carl?

CARL. O.K. Make it whole wheat. (*Elma gets soda from re-frigerator, takes it to Dr. Lyman.*)

DR. LYMAN. (*To Elma, as she brings him more soda.*) Yes, I am free. My third and last wife deserted me several years ago . . . for a ballplayer. (*He chuckles as though it were all a big absurdity.*)

ELMA. (*Starts back to counter, stops. A little astounded.*) Your third? (*Grace makes sandwich, gives it and coffee to Carl, stands behind counter talking to him as he eats.*)

DR. LYMAN. (*Elma sits at his table.*) Yes, my third! Getting married is a careless habit I've fallen into. Sometime, really, I *must* give it all up. Oh, but she was pretty! Blonde, like the young lady over there. (*He indicates Cherie.*) And southern, too, or pretended to be. However, she was kinder than the others when we parted. She didn't care about money. All she wanted was to find new marital bliss with her ballplayer, so I never had to pay her alimony . . . as if I could. (*He chuckles, sighs and recalls another.*) My second wife was a different type entirely. But she was very pretty, too. I have always exercised the most excellent taste, if not the best judgment. She was a student of mine, when I was teaching at an eastern university. Alas! she sued me for divorce on the grounds that I was incontinent and always drunk. (*Elma rises, starts L.*) I didn't have

16

a chance to resign from that position. (*Still he manages to chuckle about it.*)

CHERIE. (*From the counter.*) Hey! how much are them dough- /.12
nuts? (*She is counting the coins in her purse.*)

ELMA. (*Leaving Dr. Lyman, hurrying back to counter.*) I'll make you a special price, two for a nickel.

CHERIE. O.K.

DR. LYMAN. (*Musingly he begins to recite as though for his own enjoyment.*)

> "That time of year thou may'st in me behold
> When yellow leaves, or none, or few, do hang
> Upon those boughs ——"

CHERIE. (*She shivers, Elma hands her doughnuts on a plate, Cherie gives Elma money and crosses to stove.*) I never was so cold in my life.

ELMA. Do you honestly work in a night club?

CHERIE. (*Brightening with this recognition.*) Sure! I'm a chanteuse. I call m'self Cherie.

ELMA. That's French, isn't it?

CHERIE. I dunno. I jest seen the name once and it kinda appealed t' me.

ELMA. It's French. It means "dear one." Is that all the name you use?

CHERIE. (*Sits at a table.*) Sure. Thass all the name ya need. Like Hildegarde. She's a chanteuse, too.

ELMA. (*Crosses to Cherie with coffee.*) Chanteuse means singer.

CHERIE. How come *you* know so much? (*Grace sits at counter with Carl.*)

ELMA. I'm taking French in high school.

CHERIE. Oh! (*A reflective pause.*) I never got as far as high school. See, I was the oldest girl left in the fam'ly after my sister Violet ran away. I had two more sisters, both younger'n me, and five brothers, most of 'em older. Was they mean! Anyway, I had to quit school when I was twelve, to stay home and take care a the house and do the cookin'. I'm a real good cook. Honest!

ELMA. (*Sits L. of Cherie at table.*) Did you study singing?

CHERIE. (*Shaking her head.*) Huh-uh. Jest picked it up listenin' to the radio, seein' movies, tryin' to put over my songs as good as them people did.

ELMA. How did you get started in the night club?

17

CHERIE. I won a amateur contest. Down in Joplin, Missouri. I won the second prize there . . . a coupla boys won *first* prize . . . they juggled milk bottles . . . I don't think that's fair, do you? To make an artistic performer compete with jugglers and knife-throwers and people like that?

ELMA. No, I don't.

CHERIE. Anyway, second prize was good enough to get me to Kanz City t'enter the contest there. It was a real *big* contest and I didn't win any prize at all, but it got me the job at the Blue Dragon.

ELMA. Is that where you're from, Joplin? (*Dr. Lyman is reading a book.*)

CHERIE. (*With an acceptance of nature's catastrophes.*) No. Joplin's a *big* town. I lived 'bout a hundred miles from there, in River Gulch, a li'l town in the Ozarks. I lived there till the floods come, three years ago this spring and washed us all away.

ELMA. Gee, that's too bad.

CHERIE. I dunno where any a my folks are now, 'cept my baby sister Nan. We all just separated when the floods come and I took Nan into Joplin with me. She got a job as a waitress and I went to work in Liggett's drug store, 'til the amateur contest opened.

ELMA. It must be fun working in a night club.

CHERIE. (*A fleeting look of disillusionment comes over her face.*) Well . . . it ain't all roses.

CARL. (*Leaving Grace for the moment, crosses to Will, gets his coat.*) You gonna be here a while, Will?

WILL. I reckon. (*Elma rises, crosses to below counter.*)

CARL. I'm gonna send them cowboys in here now, and leave *you* to look after 'em.

WILL. I'll do my best.

CARL. Tell ya somethin' else, Will. (*Carl looks at Dr. Lyman cautiously, as though he didn't want to be overheard by him, then moves very closely to Will and whispers something in his ear. Will looks very surprised.*)

WILL. I'll be jiggered.

CARL. So, ya better keep an eye on *him*, too. (*Starts off.*)

WILL. Ain't you comin' back, Carl?

CARL. (*Obviously he is faking, and a look between him and Grace tells us something is up between them. He winks at her and*

18

stretches.) To tell the truth, Will, I git so darn *stiff,* sittin' at the wheel all day, I thought I'd go out fer a long walk.

WILL. In this blizzard? You gone crazy? (*Elma is doing dishes behind the counter.*)

CARL. No. That's just the kinda fella I am, Will. I like to go fer long walks in the rain and snow. Freshens a fella up. Sometimes I walk fer hours. (*Grace clears dishes from counter.*)

WILL. Ya do?

CARL. Yah. Fer hours. That's just the kinda fella I am. (*He saunters out R. now, whistling to show his nonchalance.*)

WILL. (*Rises, crosses L. to counter. To Grace.*) Imagine! Goin' out fer a walk, a night like this.

GRACE. Well, it's really very good for one, Will. It really is.

CHERIE. (*Crosses L. to counter carrying coffee and doughnuts, sits on stool and leans over counter to talk to Elma privately.*) He said he was gonna wake him up. Then he'll be in here pretty soon. You won't let on I said anything 'bout him, will ya? (*Will sits near stove, reads newspaper.*)

ELMA. No. Cross my heart. (*Dr. Lyman is suddenly reminded of another poem, which he begins to recite in full voice as he rises.*)

DR. LYMAN.

> "Shall I compare thee to a Summer's day?
> Thou art more lovely and more temperate:
> Rough winds do shake the darling buds of May,
> And Summer's lease hath all too short a date."

ELMA. (*Still behind counter, she hears Dr. Lyman, smiles fondly, and calls to him across room.*) Why, that's one of my favorite sonnets.

DR. LYMAN. It is? Do you read Shakespeare? (*Grace crosses to Dr. Lyman's table, which she clears, taking dishes back to counter. Dr. Lyman is at counter.*)

ELMA. I studied him at school, in English class. I loved the sonnets. I memorized some of them myself.

DR. LYMAN. (*Sits on stool.*) I used to know them all, by heart. And many of the plays I could recite in their entirety. I often did, for the entertainment and the annoyance of my friends. (*He and Elma laugh together.*)

ELMA. Last fall I memorized the Balcony Scene from *Romeo and Juliet.* A boy in class played Romeo and we presented it for convocation one day.

19

DR. LYMAN. Ah! I wish I had been there to see. (*Cherie feels called upon to explain her own position in regard to Shakespeare, as Elma resumes work behind counter. Grace crosses to sink, washes dishes.*)

CHERIE. Where I went to school, we din read no Shakespeare 'til the ninth grade. In the ninth grade everyone read *Julius Caesar*. I oney got as far as the eighth. I seen Marlon Brando in the movie, though. I sure do like that Marlon Brando.

DR. LYMAN. (*Now that Cherie has called attention to herself.*) Madam, where is thy Lochinvar?

CHERIE. (*Giggling.*) I don't understand anything you say, but I just love the way you say it.

DR. LYMAN. And *I* . . . understand *everything* I say . . . but privately despise the way I say it.

CHERIE. (*Giggling.*) That's so cute. (*A memory returns.*) I had a very nice friend once that recited poetry.

DR. LYMAN. (*With spoofing seriousness.*) Whatever could have happened to him?

CHERIE. I dunno. He left town. His name was Mr. Everett Brubaker. He sold second-hand cars at the corner of Eighth and Wyandotte. He had a lovely Pontiac car-with-the-top-down. He talked nice, but I guess he really wasn't any nicer'n any of the others.

DR. LYMAN. The others?

CHERIE. Well . . . ya meet quite a few men in the place I worked at, the Blue Dragon night club, out by the stockyards. Ever hear of it?

DR. LYMAN. No, and I deeply regret the fact.

CHERIE. You're just sayin' that. An educated man like you, you wouldn't have no use fer the Blue Dragon.

l. 15   DR. LYMAN. (*With a dubious look.*) I wouldn't? (*The front door swings open again and the two cowboys, Bo Decker and Virgil Blessing, enter. Virgil enters first, crosses U. L. C. Bo stands inside door R., looks around. Cherie moves D. L. Their appearance now is rumpledly picturesque and they both could pass, at first glance, for outlaws. Bo is in his early twenties, is tall and slim and good looking in an outdoors way. Now he is very unkempt. He wears faded jeans that cling to his legs like shedding skin, his boots, worn under his jeans, are scuffed and dusty, and the Stetson on the back of his head is worn and tattered. Over a faded deni*

20

shirt he wears a shiny horsehide jacket, and around his neck is
tied a bandana. Virgil is a man in his forties who seems to regard
Bo in an almost parental way. A big man, corpulent and slow
moving, he seems almost an adjunct of Bo. Dressed similarly to
Bo, perhaps a trifle more tidy, he carries a guitar in a case and
keeps a bag of Bull Durham in his shirt pocket, out of which he
rolls frequent cigarettes. Both men are still trying to wake up
from their snooze, but Bo is quick to recognize Cherie. Neither
cowboy has thought to shut the door behind them and the others
begin to shiver.)

BO. (In a full voice accustomed to speaking in an open field.)
Hey! Why din anyone wake us up? Virg'n I mighta froze out
there.

GRACE. Hey! Shut the door.

BO. (Calling across the room.) Cherry! how come you get off the
bus, 'thout lettin' me know? That any way to treat the man you're
gonna marry?

WILL. (Lifting his eyes from the paper.) Shut the door, cowboy!
(Bo doesn't even hear Will, but strides across the room to Cherie,
who is huddled over the counter as though hoping he might overlook her. Virgil, still rubbing sleep out of his eyes, drifts near the
stove.)

BO. Thass no way to treat a fella, Cherry, to slip off the bus like
ya wanted to get rid of him, maybe. And come in here and eat by
yourself. I thought we'd have a li'l snack t'gether. Sometimes I
don't understand you, Cherry.

CHERIE. Fer the hunderth time, my name ain't Cherry.

BO. I cain't say it the way you do. What's wrong with Cherry?

CHERIE. It's kinda embarrassin'.

WILL. (In a firmer, louder voice.) Cowboy, will you have the
decency to shut that door! (Virgil now responds immediately,
crosses R. and quickly closes the door as Bo turns to Will.)

BO. (There is nothing to call him for the moment but insolent
as he crosses U. R. C. to Will.) Why, what's the matter with you,
Mister? You afraid of a little fresh air? (Will glowers but Bo is
not fazed.) Why, man, ya oughta breathe real deep and git yor
lungs full of it. Thass the trouble with you city people. You git soft.
(Will rises, comes L. of Bo.)

VIRGIL. (Whispering.) He's the sheriff, Bo.

BO. (In full voice, for Will's benefit.) S'posin' he is the sheriff!

What's that matter t' *me*? That don't give him the right t' insult my manners, does it? No man ever had to tell *me* what t' do, did he, Virge? Did he?

VIRGIL. No. No. But there allus comes a time, Bo, when . . . *(Virgil puts his guitar down, Bo puts his hat on top of it.)*

BO. *(Ignoring Virgil, speaking out for the benefit of all.)* My name's Bo Decker. I'm twenty-one years old and own me m'own ranch up in Timber Hill, Montana, where I got a herd a fine Hereford cattle and a dozen horses, and the finest sheep and hogs and chickens anywhere in the country. And I jest come back from a rodeo where I won 'bout ev'ry prize there *was*, din I, Virge? *(Joshingly, he elbows Virgil in the ribs. Will drifts D. S., looking at Bo.)* Yap, I'm the prize bronco-buster, 'n steer-roper, 'n bull-dogger, anywhere 'round. I won 'em all. And what's more, had my picture taken by *Life* magazine. *(Confronting Will.)* So I'd appreciate your talkin' to me with a little respect in yor voice, Mister, and not go hollerin' orders to me from across the room like I was some no-count servant. *(Will is flabbergasted.)*

CHERIE. *(Privately to Elma.)* Did ya ever see anybody like him?

WILL. *(Finally finds his voice and uses it, after a struggle with himself to sound just and impartial.)* You was the last one in, cowboy, and you left the door open. You shoulda closed it, I don't care *who* y'are. That's all I'm saying.

1.16 BO. Door's closed now. What ya arguin' 'bout? *(Leaving a bushed and somewhat awed audience, Bo strides over to the counter and drops to a stool.)* Seems like we're gonna be here a while, Virge. How's fer some grub? *(Will turns U. C.)*

VIRGIL. *(Remaining by magazine counter.)* Not yet, Bo. I'm chewin' t'backy. *(Takes off coat and hat.)*

BO. *(Slapping a thigh.)* Thass ole Virge for ya. Allus happy long's he's got a wad a t'backy in his mouth. Wall, I'm gonna have me a li'l snack. *(To Elma.)* Miss, gimme 'bout three hamburgers.

ELMA. Three? How do you want them? *(Will crosses to stove, watches Bo.)*

BO. I want 'em *raw*. *(Cherie makes a sick face. Dr. Lyman quietly withdraws, taking his drink over to the window.)*

ELMA. Honest?

BO. It's the only way t'eat 'em, raw, with a thick slice a onion and some pickalili.

ELMA. *(Hesitant.)* Well . . . if you're sure you're not joking.

22

BO. (*His voice holding Elma on her way to refrigerator.*) Jest a
minute, Miss. That ain't all. I'd also like me some ham and eggs
. . . and some potaty salad . . . and a piece a pie. I ain't so
pertikler what kinda pie it is, so long as it's got that murang on
top of it. (*Grace gives hamburger and eggs to Elma.*)
ELMA. We have lemon and choc'late. They both have meringue.
(*Virgil crosses* U. S., *sits near stove. Grace crosses* U. R., *sits on
bench.*)
BO. (*Thinking it over.*) Lemon'n choc'late. I like 'em both. I
dunno which I'd ruther have. (*Ponders a moment.*) I'll have 'em
both, Miss. (*Cherie makes another sick face.*)
ELMA. Both?
BO. Yep! 'N set a quart a milk beside me. I'm still a growin' boy. 1.16A
(*Elma starts preparations as Bo turns to Cherie.*) Travelin' allus
picks up my appetite. That all you havin', jest a measly doughnut?
CHERIE. I ain't hungry.
BO. Why not?
CHERIE. I jest ain't.
BO. Ya oughta be.
CHERIE. Well—I ain't!
BO. Wait till I get ya up to the Susie-Q. I'll fatten ya up. I bet in
two weeks time, ya won't recognize yorself. (*Now he puts a* 1.16B
*bearlike arm around her, drawing her close to him for a snuggle,
kissing her on the cheek.*) But doggone, I love ya, Cherry, jest
the way ya are. Yor about the cutest li'l piece I ever did see. And
man! when I walked into that night club place and hear you singin'
my favorite song, standin' before that orkester lookin' like a angel,
I told myself then and there, she's fer *me*. I ain't gonna leave this
place without her. And now I got ya, ain't I, Cherry?
CHERIE. (*Trying to avoid his embrace.*) Bo . . . there's people
here . . . they're lookin' . . . (*And she's right. They are.*)
BO. What if they are? It's no crime to show a li'l affection, is it?
'Specially, when we're gonna git married. It's no crime I ever
heard of. (*He squeezes her harder now and forces a loud, smack-
ing kiss on the lips. Cherie twists loose of him and turns away.*)
CHERIE. Bo! fer cryin' out loud, lemme *be!* (*Breaks away* R.)
BO. (*Following her, grabs her shoulders.*) Cherry, thass no way
to talk to yor husband.
CHERIE. (*Breaks away* R. C.) That's all ya done since we left
Kanz City, is maul me. (*Sits at table.*)

23

BO. Oh, is zat so? (*This is a deep-cutting insult.*) Wall, I cei-
tainly ain't one to *pester* any woman with my affections. I never
had to *beg* no woman to make love to me. (*Calling over his
shoulder to Virgil.*) Did I, Virge? I never had to coax no woman
to make love to me, *did* I?

VIRGIL. (*In a voice that sounds more and more restrained.*) No
. . . no . . .

BO. (*Still in full voice.*) No! Ev'rywhere I go, I got all the
wimmin I want, don't I, Virge? I gotta fight 'em to keep 'em off
me, don't I, Virge? (*Virgil is saved from having to make a response
as Elma presents Bo with his hamburgers.*)

ELMA. Here are the hamburgers. The ham and eggs will take a
little longer.

BO. (*Sits at counter, eats.*) O.K. These'll gimme a start. (*Grace
rubs her forehead with a feigned expression of pain.*)

GRACE. (*Rises, crosses L. to U. S. end of counter.*) Elma, honey,
I got the darndest headache.

ELMA. I'm sorry, Grace.

GRACE. Can you look after things a while?

ELMA. Sure.

GRACE. 'Cause the only thing for me to do is go upstairs and lie
down a while. That's the only thing gonna do me any good at all.
(*Starts U. L.*)

WILL. (*From his chair.*) What's the matter, Grace?

GRACE. (*At the rear door.*) I got a headache, Will, that's just
drivin' me *wild*.

WILL. That so? (*Grace goes out rear door.*)

DR. LYMAN. (*Crosses to U. S. end of counter. To Elma.*) You
are now the Mistress of the Inn.

ELMA. You haven't told me anything about your first wife.

DR. LYMAN. (*To D. S. end of counter.*) Now, how could I have
omitted her?

ELMA. What was *she* like? (*Bo eats, peeks at Cherie now and
then.*)

DR. LYMAN. (*Still in the highest of spirits.*) Oh . . . she was
the loveliest of them all. I do believe she was. We had such an
idyllic honeymoon together, a golden month of sunshine and romance, in Bermuda. (*Sits on stool. Elma leans on counter.*) She
sued me for divorce later, on the grounds of mental cruelty, and
persuaded the judge that she should have my house and my motor-

24

car, and an alimony that I still find it difficult to pay, for she never chose to marry again. She found that for all she wanted out of marriage, she didn't have to marry. (*He chuckles.*) Ah, but perhaps I am being unkind. (*Elma is a little mystified by the humor with which he always tells of his difficulties. Bo now leans over the counter and interrupts.*) 1 19

BO. Miss, was you waitin' fer me to lay them eggs?

ELMA. (*Hurrying to stove.*) Oh, I'm sorry. They're ready now. (*Bo jumps up, grabs a plate and glides over the counter for Elma to serve him from the stove.*)

BO. Them hamburgers was just a *horse d'oovrey.* (*He grins with appreciation of this word. Elma fills his plate.*) Thank ya, Miss. (*He starts back for the stool but trips over Cherie's suitcase on the way.*) Daggone! (*He looks down to see what has stopped him. Cherie holds a rigid silence. Bo brings his face slowly up, looking at Cherie suspiciously. Puts plate of eggs on counter.*) Cherry! (*She says nothing. He crosses slowly toward her.*) Cherry, what'd ya wanta bring yor suitcase in here fer? (*She still says nothing.*) Cherry, I'm askin' ya a civil question. What'd ya bring yor suitcase in fer? Tell me? (*Will rises.*)

CHERIE. (*Frightened, rises.*) I . . . I . . . now don't you come near me, Bo. (*Backs R.*)

BO (*Crosses, shaking Cherie by the shoulders.*) Tell me! What's yor suitcase doin' there b'hind the counter? What were ya tryin' to do, fool me? Was you plannin' to git away from me? That what you been sittin' here plannin' t'do?

CHERIE. (*Finding it hard to speak while he is shaking her.*) Bo . . . lemme be . . . take your hands off me, Bo Decker.

BO. Tell me, Cherry. Tell me. (*Now Will intercedes, coming up 1. 19 A to Bo, laying a hand on his shoulder.*)

WILL. Leave the little lady alone, cowboy.

BO. (*Turning on Will fiercely. Cherie backs R.*) Mister, ya got no right interferin' 'tween me and my feeancy.

WILL. Mebbe she's yor feeancy and maybe she ain't. Anyway, ya ain't gonna abuse her while I'm here. Unnerstand?

BO. *Abuse* her?

WILL. (*To Cherie.*) I think you better tell him now, Miss, jest how you feel about things. (*Bo looks at Cherie with puzzled wonder.*)

CHERIE. (*Finding it impossible to say.*) I . . . I . . .

25

BO. What's this critter tryin' to say, Cherry?

CHERIE. Well . . . I . . .

WILL. You better tell him, Miss.

CHERIE. Now, Bo, don't git mad.

BO. I'll git mad if I feel like it. What you two got planned?

CHERIE. Bo, I don't wanta go up to Montana and marry ya.

BO. Ya do, too.

CHERIE. I do not!

BO. (*Crosses* L. *a few steps.*) Anyways, you'll come to like it in time. I *promised* ya would. Now we been through all that b'fore. (*Will sits on stool at counter.*)

CHERIE. But, Bo . . . I ain't goin'.

BO. (*A loud blast of protest.*) *What?* (*Cherie runs* U. L.)

CHERIE. I ain't goin'. The sheriff here said he'd help me. He ain't gonna let you take me any farther. I'm stayin' here and take the next bus back to Kanz City.

BO. (*Crosses* U. L. *Grabbing her by the shoulders to reassure himself of her.*) You ain't gonna do nothin' of the kind.

CHERIE. Yes, I am, Bo. You gotta b'lieve me. I ain't goin' with ya. That's final.

BO. (*In a most personal voice, baffled.*) But, Cherry . . . we was *familiar* with each other.

CHERIE. That don't mean ya gotta *marry* me.

BO. (*Shocked at her, steps back.*) Why . . . I oughta take you across my knee and blister yer li'l bottom.

CHERIE. (*More frightened, runs* D. L.) Don't you touch me.

BO. (*To Will, crosses* L. *a step.*) You cain't pay no tension to what she says, Mister. Womenfolk don't know their own minds. Never did. (*Cherie runs* R. *near door, Bo follows.*)

CHERIE. Don't you come near me!

BO. (*Crosses* R. *to Cherie.*) Yor gonna follow me back to Timber Hill and marry up. You just think you wouldn't like it now 'cause ya never been there and the whole idea's kinda strange. But you'll get over them feelin's. In no time at all, yor gonna be happy as a mudhen. I ain't takin' *no* fer an answer. By God, yor comin' along. (*He grabs her forcefully to him, as Will interferes again, pulling the two apart.*)

WILL. You're not takin' her with ya if she don't wanta go. Can't you get that through your skull? Now leave her be. (*Bo stands*

26

looking at Will with sullen hatred. Cherie trembles and backs R. *Virgil stands far* R. *looking apprehensive.*)

BO. (*Confronts Will threateningly.*) This ain't no bizness of yors.

WILL. It's my business when the little lady comes t'me wantin' protection.

BO. Is that right, Cherry? (*She steps back, as he steps toward her.*) Did you go to the sheriff askin' fer pertection?

CHERIE. (*Meekly, backs away another step.*) . . . yes, I guess I did.

BO. (*Bellowing out again.*) Why? What'd ya need pertection for . . . from a man that wants to marry ya?

CHERIE. (*Shuddering.*) . . . 'cause . . .

BO. (*Bellowing angrily.*) 'Cause why? I said I loved ya, din I?

CHERIE. (*About to cry.*) I know ya did.

BO. (*Confronting Will with a feeling of angry unjustness.*) See there? I told her I loved her and I wanta marry her. And with a world fulla crazy people goin' 'round killin' each other, you ain't got nothin' better t'do than stand here tryin' to keep me from it. (*Turns away* R.)

WILL. Yor overlookin' jest one thing, cowboy.

BO. (*With gruff impatience.*) Yor so smart. Tell me what I'm overlookin'.

WILL. Yor overlookin' the simple but important fack that the little lady don't love you. (*Bo now is trapped into silence. He can say nothing, and one can tell that Will has named a fact that Bo did not intend to face. Virgil watches him alertly. He can tell that Bo is angry enough to attack Will and is about to. Virgil hurries to Bo's side, holding his arms as though to restrain him. Dr. Lyman rises, Elma starts* U. L. *for Grace, then stops.*)

VIRGIL. (*Pacifyingly, pulls Bo* R.) Now, Bo. Take it easy, Bo. Don't blow your lid. He's the sheriff, Bo. Hold yor temper.

BO. (*To Virgil.*) That polecat bastard! He said she din love me.

VIRGIL. (*Trying to draw him away from the scene over to* R.) Pay no 'tention, Bo. Come on over here and sit down. Ya gotta think things over, Bo.

BO. (*Twisting loose from Virgil's hold, walks* D. L.) Lemme be, Virge.

WILL. Ask the li'l lady, if ya don't b'lieve me. Ask her if she loves ya.

BO. I won't ask her nothin' of the kind.

WILL. All right then, take my word for it.

BO. I wouldn't take yor word for a cloudy day. I'm tellin' ya, she loves me. And I oughta know. (*Starts toward Cherie. Virgil goes* R. *Cherie flees to the counter, sobbing.*)

WILL. (*Stops Bo.*) Wall . . . she ain't gettin' back on the bus with ya. We'll leave it at that. So you better take my advice and sit down with yor friend there, and have a quiet game a pinochle till the bus gets on its way and takes you with it.

VIRGIL. Do like he tells ya, Bo. I think mebbe ya got the li'l lady all wrong, anyway. (*Near a table* R.)

BO. (*A defender of womanhood.*) Don't you say nothin' against her, Virge.

VIRGIL. I *ain't* sayin' nothin' *against* her. I jest see no reason why you should marry a gal that says she don't love ya. That's all. And I kinda doubt she's as good a gal as you think she is. Now come on over here and sit down. (*Sits at table.*)

1.19c BO. (*Turns restlessly from Virgil.*) I don't feel like sittin'. (*Instead, he paces up to the big window, standing there looking out, his back to the audience. Will gets coat and hat.*)

ELMA. (*From behind counter, to Virgil.*) What shall I do with the ham and eggs?

VIRGIL. Just put 'em on the stove and keep 'em warm, Miss. He'll have 'em a li'l later. (*She puts plate on hot plate.*)

WILL. (*To Cherie.*) I don't think you'll be bothered any more, Miss. If y'are, my station's right across the road. You kin holler. (*Dr. Lyman returns to counter, sits.*)

CHERIE. (*Dabbing at her eyes.*) Thank you very much, I'm sure.

WILL. Are you gonna be all right, Elma?

ELMA. (*Surprised at the question.*) Why, yes, Will! (*Will just looks at Dr. Lyman who, we can tell, is made to feel a little uncomfortable.*)

WILL. I'll look in a little later.

1.20 ELMA. O.K., Will. (*Will goes to the front door, takes a final look at Bo, then goes out.*)

DR. LYMAN. I don't know why, but . . . I always seem to relax more easily . . . when a sheriff leaves the room. (*He chuckles bravely. Cherie drifts to* D. L. *end of counter, sits on stool.*)

ELMA. I think it's awfully unfair that people dislike Will just because he's a sheriff.

DR. LYMAN. But you see, my dear, he stands as a symbol of

28

authority, the most dreaded figure of our time. Policemen, teac' ers, lawyers, judges, doctors, and I suppose, even tax collectors . . . we take it for granted that they are going to punish us for something we didn't do . . . or did do.

ELMA. But you said you were a teacher once.

DR. LYMAN. But not a successful one. I could never stay in one place very long at a time. And I hated having anyone *over* me, like deans and presidents and department heads. I never was a man who could take *orders* . . . from *anyone* . . . without feeling resentment. Right or wrong, I have always insisted on having my own way. (*Pours a drink. Bo walks slowly down from his corner retreat, seeking Virgil, who is taking his guitar out of its case. Bo speaks hesitantly in a low voice.*)

BO. What am I gonna do, Virge?

VIRGIL. Bo, ya just gotta quit dependin' on me so much. I don't know what to tell ya to do, except to sit down and be peaceful.

BO. I—I can't be peaceful. (*Moves L.*)

VIRGIL. All right then, pace around like a panther and be miserable.

BO. (*To himself. Turns R.*) I—I jest can't believe it!

VIRGIL. *What* can't ya believe?

BO. (*Now he becomes embarrassed. Crosses D. R.*) Oh . . . nothin'.

VIRGIL. If ya got anything on your chest, Bo, it's best to get it off.

BO. (*Sits at table by Virgil.*) Well, I . . . I just never realized . . . a gal might not . . . love me.

CURTAIN

ACT II

Only a few minutes have elapsed since the close of Act I. Our characters now are patiently trying to pass the time as best they can. Virgil has taken out his guitar and, after tuning it, begun to play a soft, melancholy cowboy ballad as he sits at the same table. He keeps his music an almost unnoticeable part of the background. Bo lingers in the corner up R., a picture of troubled dejection. Cherie has found a movie magazine which she sits at one of the tables and reads. Dr. Lyman continues sitting at the bar, sipping his drink and courting Elma, although Elma does not realize she is being courted. She is immensely entertained by him. She sits on a stool behind counter.

ELMA. . . . and where else did you teach?

DR. LYMAN. My last position was at one of those revolting little progressive colleges in the East, where they offer a curriculum of what they call *functional* education. Educators, I am sure, have despaired of ever teaching students *anything*, so they have decided the second-best thing to do is to *understand* them. (*Bo sits on bench by window.*) Every day there would be a meeting of everyone on the entire faculty, with whom the students ever came into any contact, from the President down to the chambermaids, and we would put our collective heads together to try to figure out why little Jane or little Mary was not getting out of her classes what she *should*. The suggestion that perhaps she wasn't studying was too simple, and if you implied that she simply did not have the brains for a college education, you were being undemocratic.

ELMA. You must have disapproved of that college.

DR. LYMAN. My dear girl, I have disapproved of my entire life.

ELMA. Really?

DR. LYMAN. Yes, but I suppose I couldn't resist living it over again. (*There is a touch of sadness about him now.*)

ELMA. Did you resign from that position?

DR. LYMAN. One day I decided I had had enough. I walked blithely into the Dean's office and said, "Sir! I graduated *Magna*

30

Cum Laude from the University of Chicago, I studied at Oxford on a Rhodes Scholarship, and returned to take my Ph.D. at Harvard, receiving it with highest honors. I think I have the right to expect my students to try to understand *me*."

ELMA. (*Very amused.*) What did he say?

DR. LYMAN. Oh, I didn't wait for a response. I walked out of the door and went to the railroad station, where I got a ticket for the farthest place I could think of, which happened to be Las Vegas. And I have been traveling ever since. It's a merry way to go to pot. (*He chuckles.*)

ELMA. I had thought I might teach one day, but you don't make it sound very attractive.

DR. LYMAN. Ah, suit yourself. Don't let me influence you one way or the other. (*Elma smiles and Dr. Lyman gives in to the sudden compulsion of clasping her hand.*) You're a lovely young girl.

ELMA. (*Very surprised.*) Why . . . thank you, Dr. Lyman.

DR. LYMAN. (*Clears his throat and makes a fresh approach.*) Did you tell me you plan to go to Topeka tomorrow?

ELMA. (*Looking at clock. Removes hand.*) You mean today. Yes. I have a ticket to hear the Kansas City Symphony. They come to Topeka every year to give a concert.

DR. LYMAN. (*Feeling his way.*) You say . . . you stay with your sister there?

ELMA. (*Rises.*) Yes, then I take an early morning bus back here, in time for school Monday. Then after school, I come here to work for Grace.

DR. LYMAN. (*Obviously he is angling for something.*) Didn't you say there was a university in Topeka?

ELMA. Yes. Washburn University.

DR. LYMAN. Washburn University—of course! You know, it just occurs to me that I should stop there to check some references on a piece of research I'm engaged on.

ELMA. Oh, I've been to Washburn library lots of times.

DR. LYMAN. You have? (*He shows some cunning, but obviously Elma does not see it.*) Perhaps you would take me there!

ELMA. (*Hesitant.*) Well, I . . .

DR. LYMAN. I'll arrive in Topeka before you do, then meet your bus . . .

ELMA. If you really want me to.

DR. LYMAN. You can take me to the library, then perhaps we

could have dinner together, and perhaps you would permit me to take you to the symphony.

ELMA. (Overjoyed.) Are you serious?

DR. LYMAN. Why, of course I'm serious. Why do you ask?

ELMA. I don't know. Usually, older people are too busy to take notice of kids. I'd just love to.

DR. LYMAN. Then I may depend on it that I have an engagement?

ELMA. Yes. Oh, that'll be lots of fun. I can't wait.

DR. LYMAN. But, my dear . . . let's not tell anyone of our plans, shall we? (Cherie rises, crosses R and puts magazine back in rack. Bo rises, expectant. Cherie stands near door, watching Virgil.)

ELMA. Why not?

DR. LYMAN. You see . . . I have been married, and I am somewhat older than you, though perhaps not quite as old as you might take me to be . . . anyway, people might not understand.

ELMA. Oh!

DR. LYMAN. So let's keep our plans to ourselves. Promise?

ELMA. O.K. If you think best.

DR. LYMAN. (Rises. Pats her hand. Crosses R. to book rack, looks at books, Elma sits, knits.) I think it best. (Virgil has finished playing a ballad and Cherie applauds.)

CHERIE. That was real purty, Virgil.

VIRGIL. Thank ya, Miss. (From his corner, Bo has seen the moment's intimacy between them. He winces. Cherie goes over to the counter and speaks to Elma.)

CHERIE. Isn't there some other way of me gettin' back to Kanz City?

ELMA. I'm sorry. The bus comes through here from Topeka, and it can't get through, either, until the road's cleared.

CHERIE. I was jest gettin' sorta restless. (She sits at center table and lights a cigarette. Suddenly, the front door swings open and Will appears carrying a thermos jug.)

WILL. (Crossing to counter.) Elma, fill this up for me, like a good girl.

ELMA. Sure, Will. (Takes thermos from him and starts to fill it at urn.)

WILL. I'm goin' down the highway a bit to see how the men are gettin' on. Thought they'd enjoy some hot coffee.

ELMA. Good idea, Will.

WILL. (*With a look around.*) Everyone behavin'?

ELMA. Of course.

WILL. (*Puzzled.*) Grace not down yet?

ELMA. No.

WILL. I didn't see Carl any place outside. Suppose somethin' coulda happened to him?

ELMA. I wouldn't worry about him, Will.

WILL. I s'pose he can take care of himself. (*Elma hands him thermos.*) Thank you, Elma. (*He pays her, then starts back out, saying for the benefit primarily of Bo and Dr. Lyman.*) Oh, Elma. If anyone should be wantin' me, I won't be gone very long. (*He looks around to make sure everyone has heard him, then goes out front door. Bo has heard and seen him, and suddenly turns from his corner and comes angrily down to Virgil. Dr. Lyman drifts to window and sits.*) 2.4

BO. That dang sheriff! If it wasn't fer *him*, I'd git Cherry now and . . . I . . .

VIRGIL. Where would ya take her, Bo?

BO. There's a justice a the peace down the street. You can see his sign from the window.

VIRGIL. Bo, ya cain't *force* a gal to marry ya. Ya jest cain't do it. That sheriff's a stern man and he'd shoot ya in a minute if he saw it was his duty. Now why don't ya go over to the counter and have yourself a drink . . . like the perfessor?

BO. I never did drink and I ain't gonna let no woman drive me to it.

VIRGIL. Ya don't drink. Ya don't smoke or chew. Ya oughta have *some* bad habits to rely on when things with women go wrong. (*Bo thinks for a moment then sits opposite Virgil.*)

BO. Virge. I hate to sound like some pitiable weaklin' of a man, but there's been times the last few months, I been so lonesome, I . . . I jest didn't know what t'do with m'self.

VIRGIL. It's no disgrace to feel that way, Bo.

BO. How 'bout you, Virge? Don't you ever git lonesome, too?

VIRGIL. A long time ago, I gave up romancin' and decided I was just gonna take bein' lonesome for granted.

BO. I wish I could do that, but I cain't. (*They now sit in silence.* 2.5 *Cherie, at the counter, lifts her damp eyes to Elma seeking a confidante.*)

33

CHERIE. Mebbe I'm a sap.

ELMA. Why do you say that?

CHERIE. I dunno why I *don't* go off to Montana and marry him. I might be a lot better off'n I am now.

ELMA. He says he *loves* you.

CHERIE. He dunno what love is.

ELMA. What makes you say that?

CHERIE. All he wants is a girl to throw his arms around and hug and kiss, that's all. The resta the time, he don't even know I exist.

ELMA. What made you decide to marry him in the first place?

CHERIE. (*Giving Elma a wise look.*) Ya ain't very experienced, are ya?

ELMA. I guess not.

CHERIE. I never *did* decide to marry him. Everything was goin' fine till he brought up *that* subjeck. Bo come in one night when I was singin' "That Old Black Magic." It's one a my best numbers. And he liked it so much, he jumped up on a chair and yelled like a Indian, and put his fingers in his mouth and whistled like a steam engine. Natur'ly, it made me feel good. Most a the customers at the Blue Dragon was too drunk to pay any attention to my songs.

ELMA. And you liked him?

CHERIE. Well . . . I thought he was awful *cute*. (*She shows a mischievous smile.*)

ELMA. I think he looks a little like Burt Lancaster, don't you?

CHERIE. Mebbe. Anyway . . . I'd never seen a cowboy before. Oh, I'd seen 'em in movies, a course, but never in the *flesh* . . . Anyway, he's so darn healthy lookin', I don't mind admittin', I was attracted, right from the start.

ELMA. You were?

CHERIE. But it was only what ya might call a *sexual* attraction.

ELMA. Oh!

CHERIE. The very next mornin', he wakes up and hollers, "Yippee! We're gittin' married." (*Bo rises, walks* L. *Virgil pulls him down to sit.*) I honestly thought he was crazy. But when I tried to reason with him, he wouldn't listen to a word. He stayed by my side all day long, like a shadow. At night, a course, he had to go back to the rodeo, but he was back to the Blue Dragon as soon as the rodeo was over, in time fer the midnight show. If any other fella claimed t'have a date with me, Bo'd beat him up.

ELMA. And you never told him you'd marry him?

CHERIE. No! He kep tellin' me all week, he and Virge'd be by the night the rodeo ended, and they'd pick me up and we'd all start back to Montana t'gether. I knew that if I was around the Blue Dragon that night, that's what'd happen. So I decided to beat it. One a the other girls at the Blue Dragon lived on a farm 'cross the river in Kansas. She said I could stay with her. So I went to the Blue Dragon last night and just sang fer the first show. Then I told 'em I was quittin' . . . I'd been wantin' to find another job any-way . . . and I picked up my share of the kitty . . . but darn it, I had to go and tell 'em I was takin' the midnight bus. They had to go and tell Bo, a course, when he come in a li'l after eleven. He paid 'em five dollars to find out. So I went down to the bus station and hadn't even got my ticket, when here come Bo and Virge. (*Bo rises walks slowly to window.*) He jest steps up to the ticket window and says, "Three tickets to Montana!" I din know what to say. Then he dragged me onto the bus and I been on it ever since. And somewhere deep down inside me, I gotta funny feelin' I'm gonna end up in Montana. (*She sits now in troubled contemplation as Elma resumes her work. On the other side of the stage, Bo comes D. S., straddles a chair after a period of gestation, begins to question Virgil.*)

BO. Tell me somethin', Virge. We been t'gether since my folks died, and I allus wondered if mebbe I din spoil yer chances a settlin' down.

VIRGIL. (*Laughs.*) No, you never, Bo. I used to tell myself ya did, but I just wanted an excuse.

BO. But you been lookin' after me since I was ten.

VIRGIL. I coulda married up, too.

BO. Was ya ever in love?

VIRGIL. Oncet. B'fore I went to work on your daddy's ranch.

BO. What happened?

VIRGIL. Nuthin'.

BO. Ya ask her to marry ya?

VIRGIL. Nope.

BO. Why not?

VIRGIL. Well . . . there comes a time in every fella's life Bo, when he's gotta give up his own ways . . .

BO. How ya mean?

VIRGIL. Well, I was allus kinda uncomfortable around this gal,

35

'cause she was sweet and kinda refined. I was allus scared I'd say or do somethin' wrong.

BO. I know how ya mean.

VIRGIL. It was cowardly of me, I s'pose, but ev'ry time I'd get back from courtin' her, and come back to the bunkhouse where my buddies was sittin' around talkin', or playin' cards, or listenin' to music, I'd jest relax and feel m'self so much at home, I din wanta give it up.

BO. Yah! Gals can scare a fella.

VIRGIL. Now I'm kinda ashamed.

BO. Y'are?

VIRGIL. Yes I am, Bo. A fella can't live his whole life dependin' on buddies. (Bo takes another reflective pause, then asks directly.)

2.6A

BO. Why don't she like me, Virge?

VIRGIL. (Hesitant.) Well . . .

BO. Tell me the truth.

VIRGIL. Mebbe ya don't go about it right.

BO. What do I do wrong?

VIRGIL. Sometimes ya sound a li'l bullheaded and mean.

BO. I do?

VIRGIL. Yah.

BO. How's a fella s'posed to act?

VIRGIL. I'm no authority, Bo, but it seems t'me you should be a little more gallant.

BO. Gall—? Gallant? I'm as gallant as I know how to be. You hear the way Hank and Orville talk at the ranch, when they get back from sojournin' in town, 'bout their women.

VIRGIL. They like to brag, Bo. Ya cain't b'lieve ev'rything Hank and Orville say.

BO. Is there any reason a gal wouldn't go fer *me*, soon as she would fer Hank or Orville?

VIRGIL. They're a li'l older'n you. They learned a li'l more. They can be *gallant* with gals . . . when they *wanta* be.

BO. I ain't gonna *pertend*.

VIRGIL. I cain't blame ya.

BO. But a gal *oughta* like me. I kin read and write, I'm kinda tidy, and I got good manners, don't I?

VIRGIL. I'm no judge, Bo. I'm used to ya.

BO. And I'm tall and strong. Ain't that what girls like? And if I do say so, m'self, I'm purty good lookin'.

36

VIRGIL. Yah.

BO. When I get spruced up, I'm just as good lookin' a fella as a gal might hope to see.

VIRGIL. I know ya are, Bo.

BO. (*Suddenly seized with anger at the injustice of it all. Jumps up, crosses* U. S.) Then hellfire and damnation! Why don't she go back to the ranch with me? (*His hands in his hip pockets, he begins pacing, returning to his corner like a panther, where he stands with his back to the others, watching the snow fly outside the window.*)   2.7

ELMA. (*Having observed Bo's disquiet.*) Gee, if you only loved him!

CHERIE. That'd solve ev'rything, wouldn't it? But I don't. So I jest can't see m'self goin' to some God-forsaken ranch in Montana where I'd never see no one but him and a lotta cows.

ELMA. No. If you don't love him, it'd be awfully lonely.

CHERIE. I dunno why I keep expectin' m'self to fall in love with someone, but I do.

ELMA. (*Sits on stool by Cherie.*) I know 7 expect to, some day.

CHERIE. I'm beginnin' to seriously wonder if there *is* the kinda love I have in mind.

ELMA. What's that?

CHERIE. Well . . . I dunno. I'm oney nineteen, but I been goin' with guys since I was fourteen.

ELMA. (*Astounded.*) Honest?

CHERIE. Honey, I almost married a cousin a mine when I was fourteen, but Pappy wouldn't have it.

ELMA. I never heard of anyone marrying so young.

CHERIE. Down in the Ozarks, we don't waste much time. Anyway, I'm awful glad I never married my cousin Malcolm, 'cause he turned out real bad, like Pappy predicted. But I sure was crazy 'bout him at the time. And I been losin' my head 'bout some guy ever since. But Bo's the first one wanted to marry me, since Cousin Malcolm. And natur'ly, I'd like to get married and raise a fam'ly and all them things but . . .

ELMA. But you've *never* been in love?

CHERIE. Mebbe I have and din know it. Thass what I mean. Mebbe I don't know what love is. Mebbe I'm expectin' it t'be somethin' it ain't. I jest feel that, regardless how crazy ya are 'bout some guy, ya gotta feel . . . and it's hard to put into words,

37

but . . . ya gotta feel he *respects* ya. Yah, thass what I mean.

ELMA. (*Not impudent.*) I should think so.

CHERIE. I want a guy I can look up to and respect, but I don't want one that'll browbeat me. And I want a guy who can be sweet to me but I don't wanta be treated like a baby. I . . . I just gotta feel that . . . whoever I marry . . . has some real regard for me, apart from all the lovin' and sex. Know what I mean?

ELMA. (*Busily digesting all this.*) I think so. What are you going to do when you get back to Kansas City?

CHERIE. I dunno.—There's a hillbilly program on one a the radio stations there. I might git a job on it. If I don't, I'll prob'ly git me a job in Liggett's or Walgreen's. Then after a while, I'll prob'ly marry some guy, whether I think I love him or not. Who'm I to keep insistin' I should fall in love? You hear all about love when yor a kid and jest take it for granted that such a thing really exists. Maybe ya have to find out fer yourself it don't. Maybe everyone's afraid to tell ya.

ELMA. (*Glum.*) Maybe you're right . . . but I hope not.

CHERIE. (*After squirming a little on the stool.*) Gee, I hate to go out to that cold powder room, but I guess I better not put it off any longer. (*Cherie hurries out the rear door as Dr. Lyman sits again at the counter, having returned from the bookshelves in time to overhear the last of Cherie's conversation. He muses for a few moments, gloomily, then speaks to Elma out of his unconscious reflections.*)

DR. LYMAN. How defiantly we pursue love, like it was an inheritance due, that we had to wrangle about with angry relatives in order to get our share.

ELMA. You shouldn't complain. You've had three wives.

DR. LYMAN. Don't shame me. I loved them all . . . with passion. (*An afterthought.*) At least I thought I did . . . for a while. (*He still chuckles about it as though it were a great irony.*)

ELMA. I'm sorry if I sounded sarcastic, Dr. Lyman. I didn't mean to be.

DR. LYMAN. Don't apologize. I'm too egotistical ever to take offense at anything people *say*. (*Pours drink.*)

ELMA. You're not egotistical at all.

DR. LYMAN. Oh, believe me. The greatest egos are those which are too egotistical to show just how egotistical they are.

38

ELMA. I'm sort of idealistic about things. I like to think that people fall in love and stay that way, forever and ever.

DR. LYMAN. Maybe we have lost the ability. Maybe Man has passed the stage in his evolution wherein love is possible. Maybe life will continue to become so terrifyingly complex that man's anxiety about his mere survival will render him too miserly to give of himself in any true relation.

ELMA. You're talking over my head. *Anyone* can fall in love, I always thought . . . and . . .

DR. LYMAN. But two people, *really* in love, must give up some thing of them*selves*.

ELMA. (*Trying to follow.*) Yes.

DR. LYMAN. That is the gift that men are afraid to make. Sometimes they keep it in their bosoms forever, where it withers and dies. Then they never know love, only its facsimiles, which they seek over and over again in meaningless repetition.

ELMA. (*A little depressed.*) Gee! How did we get onto this subject?

DR. LYMAN. (*Laughs heartily with sudden release, grabbing Elma's hand.*) Ah, my dear! Pay no attention to me, for whether there is such a thing as love, we can always . . . (*Lifts his drink.*) . . . pretend there is. Let us talk instead of our forthcoming trip to Topeka. Will you wear your prettiest dress? 2.8A

ELMA. Of course. If it turns out to be a nice day, I'll wear a new dress Mother got me for spring. It's a soft rose color with a little lace collar.

DR. LYMAN. Ah, you'll look lovely, *lovely*. I know you will. I hope it doesn't embarrass you for me to speak these endearments . . .

ELMA. No . . . it doesn't embarrass me.

DR LYMAN. I'm glad. Just think of me as a fatherly old fool, will you? And not be troubled if I take such rapturous delight in your sweetness, and youth, and innocence? For these are qualities I seek to warm my heart as I seek a fire to warm my hands.

ELMA. Now I *am* kind of embarrassed. I don't know what to say.

DR. LYMAN. Then say nothing, or nudge *me* and I'll talk endlessly about the most trivial matters. (*They laugh together as* 2.9 *Cherie comes back in, shivering.*)

CHERIE. (*Crosses to stove.*) Brrr, it's cold. Virgil, I wish you'd play us another song. I think we all need somethin' to cheer us up. (*Elma crosses* D. S., *around counter.*)

2.9A VIRGIL. I'll make a deal with ya. I'll play if you'll sing.

ELMA. (*A bright idea comes to her.*) Let's have a floor show! (*Her suggestion comes as a surprise and there is silence while all consider it.*) Everyone here can do something! (*Crosses* L.)

DR. LYMAN. A brilliant idea, straight from Chaucer. You must read Juliet for me.

ELMA. (*Not hearing Dr. Lyman, running to Virgil.*) Will you play for us, Virgil? (*Cherie runs* L. *behind counter, gets suitcase, takes it* U. L. *and looks for costume.*)

VIRGIL. I don't play opery music or jitterbug.

ELMA. (*Turning to Bo.*) Will you take part? (*Stubbornly, Bo just turns the other way.*) Please! It won't be fun unless we all do something.

VIRGIL. (*Rises, crosses* L. *to* R. *of Bo.*) G'wan, Bo.

BO. I never was no play-actor, Miss.

VIRGIL. Ya kin say the Gettysburg Address.

BO. (*Gruffly.*) I ain't gonna say it now.

VIRGIL. Then why don't ya do your rope tricks? Yer rope's out on the bus. I could get it for ya easy enough.

ELMA. Oh, please! Rope tricks would be lots of fun.

BO. (*Emphatically.*) No! I ain't gonna get up before a lotta strangers and make a fool a m'self.

VIRGIL. (*To Elma.*) I guess he means it, Miss.

ELMA. Shucks! (*Crosses* D. L. *to behind counter.*)

VIRGIL. (*Quietly to Bo.*) I don't see why ya couldn't a co-operated a little, Bo.

BO. (*Rises, stands at window facing* U. S.) I got too much on my
2.9B mind to worry about doin' stunts.

ELMA. (*To Cherie.*) You'll sing a song for us, won't you, Cherie?

CHERIE. I will fer a piece a pie and another cup a coffee.

ELMA. Sure. (*Cherie hurries to Virgil.*)

CHERIE. Virgil, kin you play for me?

VIRGIL. You start me out and I think I can pick out the chords. (*Cherie sits by his side as they work out their number together. Elma hurries to Dr. Lyman.*)

ELMA. And you'll read poetry for us, won't you? (*Bo walks* D. R.)

DR. LYMAN. (*Already assuming his character.*) Why, I intend to play Romeo opposite your Juliet.

40

ELMA. Gee, I don't know if I can remember the lines.

DR. LYMAN. (*Handing her a volume he has taken off the shelves.*) Sometimes one can find Shakespeare on these shelves among the many lurid novels of juvenile delinquents. Here it is, *Four Tragedies of Shakespeare*, with my compliments. (*They begin* 2.9C *to go over the scene together as Bo, resentful of the closeness between Cherie and Virgil, goes to them belligerently.*)

BO. (*To Cherie.*) Thass my seat.

ELMA. (*Taking book from Dr. Lyman.*) If I read it over a few times, it'll come back. Do you know the Balcony Scene?

CHERIE. (*Jumping to her feet.*) You kin have it. (*Hurries to Elma, at counter.*)

DR. LYMAN. My dear, I know the entire play by heart. I can recite it backwards. (*Elma comes from behind counter to sit on stool. Dr. Lyman sits by her.*)

CHERIE. (*To Elma.*) I got a costume with me. Where can I change?

ELMA. Behind the counter. There's a mirror over the sink. (*Cherie darts behind the counter, digging into her suitcase.*)

BO. (*To Virgil.*) She shines up to you like a kitten to milk. (*Sits at Virgil's table.*)

ELMA. Gee, costumes and everything. (*She resumes her study with Dr. Lyman.*)

VIRGIL. (*Trying to make a joke of it.*) Kin I help it if I'm so darn attractive to women? (*Unfortunately Bo cannot take this as a joke, as Virgil intended. Virgil perceives he is deeply hurt.*) 2.10 Shucks, Bo, it don't mean nothin'.

BO. Maybe it don't mean nothin' to you.

VIRGIL. She was bein' nice to me 'cause I was playin' my guitar, Bo. Guitar music's kinda tender and girls seem to like it.

BO. Tender?

VIRGIL. Yah, Bo! Girls like things t' be *tender.*

BO. They do!

VIRGIL. Sure they do, Bo.

BO. A fella gets "tender," then someone comes along and makes a sap outa him.

VIRGIL. Sometimes, Bo, but not always. You just gotta take a chance.

BO. Well . . . I allus tried t' be a *decent* sorta fella, but I don't know if I'm *tender.*

VIRGIL. I think ya are, Bo. You know how ya feel about deer-huntin'. Ya never could do it. Ya couldn't any more *shoot* one a them sweet li'l deers with the sad eyes than ya could jump into boilin' oil.

BO. Are you makin' fun of me?

VIRGIL. (*Impatient with him.*) No, I'm not makin' fun of ya, Bo. I'm just tryin' to show ya that *you* got a tender side to your nature, same as anyone else.

BO. I s'pose I do.

VIRGIL. A course ya do.

BO. (*With a sudden feeling of injustice.*) Then how come Cherry don't come over and talk sweet to *me*, like she does to *you*?

VIRGIL. Ya *got* a tender side, Bo, but ya don't know how to *show* it.

BO. (*Weighing the verdict.*) I don't!

VIRGIL. No, ya just don't know how.

BO. How does a person go about showin' his tender side, Virge?

VIRGIL. Well . . . I dunno as I can tell ya. (*Elma comes over to them ready to start the show.*)

ELMA. Will you go first, Virgil?

VIRGIL. It's all right by me.

ELMA. O.K. Then I'll act as Master of the Ceremonies. (*Center-stage, to her audience.*) Ladies and gentlemen! Grace's Diner to-night presents its gala floor show of celebrated artists from all over the world! (*Virgil plays an introductory chord.*) The first number on our show tonight is that musical cowboy, Mr. Virgil—(*She pauses and Virgil supplies her with his last name.*)—Virgil Bless-ing, who will entertain you with his guitar. (*Applause. Elma retires to the back of the room where she sits on bench. Dr. Lyman crosses to sit by her. Virgil begins to play. During his playing, Bo is drawn over to the counter where he tries to further himself with Cherie, who is behind the counter, dressing.*)

BO. (*At u. s. end of counter. Innocently.*) I think you got me all wrong, Cherry.

CHERIE. Don't you come back here. (*He turns around, goes front of counter.*) I'm dressing.

BO. Cherry . . . I think you misjudged me.

CHERIE. Be quiet. (*Pops up.*) The show's started.

BO. (*Leans on counter.*) Cherry, I'm really a very *tender* person. You jest don't know. I'm so tenderhearted I don't go deer-huntin'.

42

'Cause I jest couldn't kill them "sweet li'l deers with the sad eyes."
Ask Virge.

CHERIE. I ain't int'rested. (*Ducks down.*)

BO. Ya ain't?

CHERIE. No. And furthermore I think you're a louse fer comin'
over here and talkin' while yor friend is tryin' to play the guitar.

BO. Ya talk like ya thought more a Virge than ya do a me.

CHERIE. Would ya go away and lemme alone?

BO. (*A final resort.*) Cherry, did I tell ya 'bout my color-television
set with the twenty-four-inch screen?

CHERIE. One million times! Now go 'way. (*Elma begins to make
a shushing noise to quiet Bo. Finally Bo dejectedly returns to the
other side of the room, where Virgil is just finishing his number.* 2.11B
Bo sits down at a table in the midst of Virgil's applause.)

CHERIE. That was wonderful, Virge! ⎫

DR. LYMAN. Brilliant! ⎬ (*Together.*)

ELMA. Swell! Play us another! ⎭

VIRGIL. No more just now. I'm ready to see the rest of ya do
somethin'.

BO. (*To Virgil.*) A lot *she* cares how tender I am!

ELMA. (*Coming forth again as Master of Ceremonies.*) That was
swell, Virgil. (*Turns back to Dr. Lyman.*) Are you ready?

DR. LYMAN. (*Preening himself, rises.*) I consider myself so.

ELMA. (*Taking the book to Virgil.*) Will you be our prompter?

VIRGIL. It's kinda funny writin', but I'll try.

ELMA. (*Back to Dr. Lyman above table.*) Gee, what'll we use for
a balcony?

DR. LYMAN. That offers a problem. (*Together they consider
whether to use the counter for Elma to stand on or one of the
tables.*)

BO. (*To Virgil.*) What is it these folks are gonna do, Virge?

VIRGIL. Romeo and Juliet . . . by Shakespeare! (*Puts guitar
down.*)

BO. Shakespeare!

VIRGIL. This Romeo was a great lover, Bo. Watch him and pick
up a few pointers. (*Cherie comes running out from behind the
counter now, a dressing gown over her costume, and she sits at
one of the tables.*)

CHERIE. I'm ready.

BO. (*Reading some of the lines from Virgil's book.*) "But soft

43

. . . what light through . . . yonder window breaks? It is the East . . . and Juliet is the sun . . . Arise, fair . . ." *(He has got this far only with difficulty, stumbling over most of the words. Virgil takes the book away from him now.)*

VIRGIL. Shh, Bo! *(Virgil comes forth to introduce the act as Dr. Lyman clears the counter.)*

ELMA. *(Crosses to C.)* Ladies and gentlemen! you are about to witness a playing of the balcony scene from *Romeo and Juliet.* Dr. Gerald Lyman will portray the part of Romeo, and I'll play Juliet. My name is Elma Duckworth. The scene is the orchard of the Capulets' house in Verona, Italy. *(Dr. Lyman takes a quick drink.)* This counter is supposed to be a balcony. *(Dr. Lyman helps her onto the counter where she stands, waiting for him to begin.)* O.K.? *(Dr. Lyman takes a quick reassuring drink from his bottle, then tucks it in his pocket, and comes forward in the great Romantic tradition. He is enjoying himself tremendously. The performance proves to be pure ham, but there is pathos in the fact that he does not seem to be aware of how bad he is. He is a thoroughly selfish performer, too, who reads all his speeches as though they were grand soliloquies, regarding his Juliet as a prop.)*

DR. LYMAN.
"He jests at scars, that never felt a wound.
But soft! what light through yonder window breaks?
It is the east, and Juliet is the sun!
(He tries to continue, but Elma, unmindful of cues and eager to begin her performance, reads her lines with compulsion.)
Arise . . . fair sun, and . . . kill the envious. . . ."

ELMA. *(At same time as Dr. Lyman.)*
"O Romeo, Romeo! wherefore art thou, Romeo?
Deny thy father, and refuse thy name:
Or if thou wilt not, be but sworn my love,
And I'll no longer be a Capulet."

DR. LYMAN.
"She speaks, yet she says nothing: what of that?
Her eye discourses; I will answer it.
I am too bold—"

BO. *(To Virgil.)* Bold? He's drunk.

VIRGIL. Ssssh!

DR. LYMAN.

". . . . 'tis not to me she speaks:

Two of the fairest stars in all the heaven,

Having some business, do entreat her eyes

To twinkle in their spheres till they return."

ELMA.

"Ay, me!"

DR LYMAN.

"O! speak again, bright angel; thou art

As glorious to this night, being o'er my head

As is a winged messenger of heaven

Unto the white-upturned . . ."

(Dr. Lyman continues with this speech, even though Bo talks over him.)

BO. I don't understand all them words, Virge.

VIRGE. It's *Romeo and Juliet*, for God's sake. Now will you shut up?

DR. LYMAN. (*Continuing uninterrupted.*)

". . . wondering eyes

Of mortals, that fall back to gaze on him

When he bestrides the lazy-pacing clouds,

And sails upon the bosom of the air."

(*He is getting weary but he is not yet ready to give up.*)

ELMA.

" 'Tis but thy name that is my enemy;

Thou art thyself though, not a Montague.

What's a Montague? it is not hand, nor foot,

Nor arm, nor face, or any other part

Belonging to a man. O! be some other name:

What's ——"

DR. LYMAN. (*Interrupts. Beginning to falter now. Leans on back of chair.*)

"I take thee at thy word.

Call me but love, and . . . I'll be new baptiz'd;

Henceforth . . . I never . . . will be Romeo."

(*It is as though he were finding suddenly a personal meaning in the lines.*)

ELMA.

"What man art thou, that, thus bescreen'd in night,

So stumblest on my counsel?"

DR. LYMAN. (*Beginning to feel that he cannot continue.*)
                    "By a name
I know not how to tell thee . . . who I am:
My name, dear saint, is . . . is *hateful* to myself."
(*He stops here. For several moments there is a wondering silence.
Elma signals Virgil.*)
VIRGIL. (*Prompting.*) "Because it is an enemy to thee."
DR. LYMAN. (*Leaving the scene of action, repeating the line
dumbly, making his way stumblingly back to the counter.*)
"My name . . . is hateful . . . to myself . . ."
(*Elma hurries to Dr. Lyman's side. Virgil grabs hold of Bo, pulls
him back to the floor and shames him.*)
ELMA. Dr. Lyman, what's the matter?
DR. LYMAN. My dear . . . let us not continue this meaningless
little act!
ELMA. Did I do something wrong?
DR. LYMAN. You couldn't possibly do anything wrong . . . if
you tried.
ELMA. I can try to say the lines differently.
DR. LYMAN. Don't. Don't. Just tell your audience that Romeo
suddenly is fraught with remorse. (*He drops to a stool, Elma
remaining by him a few moments, uncertainly. Bo turns to Virgil.*)
BO. Virge, if thass the way to make love . . . I'm gonna give up.
ELMA. (*Crosses R. to Virgil.*) I'm afraid he isn't feeling well.
VIRGIL. (*To Elma.*) I tried to prompt him.
ELMA. (*To herself.*) Well, we've only got one more number.
(*Crosses to Cherie.*) Are you ready?
CHERIE. (*Rises.*) Sure.
ELMA. (*Crosses R. above table.*) Ladies and gentlemen, our next
number is Mademoiselle Cherie, the international *chanteuse*, direct
from the Blue Dragon night club in Kansas City, *Cherie!* (*All
applaud as Cherie comes forth, Virgil playing an introduction for
her. Bo puts his fingers through his teeth and whistles for her.
Cherie hands her robe to Virgil. Elma clears central table, Cherie
climbs up on it.*)
CHERIE. (*Whispering to Elma.*) Remember, I don't allow no table
service during my numbers.
ELMA. O.K. (*She crosses to counter, sits on D. S. stool. In the
background now, we can observe that Dr. Lyman is drinking
heavily from the bottle in his overcoat pocket. Cherie gets up on*

46

one of the tables and begins singing her song with a chord accompaniment from Virgil. Her rendition of the song is a most dramatic one, that would seem to have been created from Cherie's observations of numerous torch-singers. But she has appeal, and if she is funny, she doesn't seem to know it. Anyway, she rekindles Bo's most fervent love, which he cannot help expressing during her performance.)

2.13B

BO. (*About the middle of the song.*) Ain't she beautiful, Virge?
VIRGIL. (*Trying to keep his mind on his playing.*) Shh, Bo!
BO. I'm gonna git her, Virge.
VIRGIL. Ssshh!
BO. (*Pause. He pays no attention to anyone.*) I made up my mind. I told myself I was gonna git me a gal. Thass the only reason I entered that rodeo, and I ain't takin' no fer an answer.
VIRGIL. Bo, will you hush up and lemme be!
BO. Anything I ever wanted in this life, I went out and got and I ain't gonna stop now. I'm gonna git her. (*The song ends now and Cherie is enraged. She jumps down from her table and while her audience applauds, she goes straight to Bo and slaps him stingingly on the face.*)

2.13C

CHERIE. You ain't got the manners God gave a monkey.
BO. (*Stunned.*) Cherry!
CHERIE. . . . and if I was a man, I'd beat the livin' daylights out of ya, and thass what some man's gonna do some day, and when it happens, I hope I'm there to see. (*She flounces back to her dressing room and crouches down behind counter, as Bo gapes. By this time Dr. Lyman has drunk himself almost to insensibility, and we see him weaving back and forth on his stool, mumbling almost incoherently.*)

2.14

DR. LYMAN. "Romeo . . . Romeo . . . wherefore art thou? Wherefore art thou . . . Romeo?" (*He laughs like a loon, falls off the stool and collapses on the floor. Elma and Virgil rush to him. Bo remains rooted, glaring at Cherie with puzzled hurt.*)
ELMA. (*Deeply concerned.*) Dr. Lyman! Dr. Lyman!
VIRGIL. The man's in a purty bad way. Let's get him on the bench. (*Elma and Virgil manage to get Dr. Lyman to his feet as Bo glides across the room, scales the counter in a leap and takes Cherie in his arms.*)

2.15

BO. I was tellin' Virge I love ya. Ya got no right to come over and slap me.

CHERIE. (*Twisting.*) Lemme be.

BO. (*Picking her up.*) We're goin' down and wake up the justice of the peace and you're gonna marry me t'night.

CHERIE. (*As he takes her in his arms and transports her to the door, just as Elma and Virgil are helping Dr. Lyman onto the bench.*) Help! Virgil, help!

BO. Shut up! I'll make ya a good husband. Ya won't never have nothin' to be sorry about.

CHERIE. (*As she is carried to the door.*) Help! Sheriff! Help me, someone! Help me! (*The action is now like that of a two-ringed circus for Elma and Virgil, whose attention suddenly is diverted from the plight of Dr. Lyman to the much noisier plight of Cherie. Bo gets her, kicking and protesting, as far as the front door when it suddenly opens and Bo finds himself confronted by Will who leaves the door open.*)

WILL. Put her down, cowboy!

BO. (*Trying to forge ahead.*) Git outta my way.

WILL. (*Shoving Bo back as Cherie manages to jump loose from his arms and runs L. behind counter.*) Yor gonna do as I say.

BO. I ain't gonna have no one interferin' in my ways. (*He makes an immediate lunge at Will, which Will is prepared for, coming up with a fist that sends Bo back reeling.*)

VIRGIL. (*Hurrying to Bo's side.*) Bo, ya cain't do this, Bo. Ya cain't pick a fight with the sheriff.

BO. (*Slowly getting back to his feet.*) By God, Mister, there ain't no man ever got the best a me, and there ain't no man ever gonna.

WILL. I'm ready and willin' to try, cowboy. Come on. (*Bo lunges at him again. Will steps aside and lets Bo send his blow into the empty doorway as he propels himself through it, outside. Then Will follows him out, where the fight continues. Virgil immediately follows them, as Elma and Cherie hurry to the window to watch.*)

CHERIE. I knowed this was gonna happen. I knowed it all along.

ELMA. Gee! I'd better call Grace. (*Starts for the rear door but Grace comes through it before she gets there. Grace happens to be wearing a dressing gown.*)

GRACE. Hey, what the hell's goin' on?

ELMA. Oh, Grace, they're fighting. Honest! It all happened so suddenly, I . . .

GRACE. (*Hurrying to R. of window. Elma stands L. of window.*) Let's see.

CHERIE. (*Leaving the window, not wanting to see any more, going to a chair by one of the tables.*) Gee, I never wanted to cause so much trouble t'anyone.

GRACE. Wow! Looks like Will's gettin' the best of him.

ELMA. (*At the window, frightened by what she sees.*) Oh!

GRACE. Yap, I'll put my money on Will Masters any time. Will's got it up here. (*Points to her head.*) Lookit that cowboy. He's green. He just swings out wild.

ELMA. (*Leaving the window. Cherie sits in chair by table.*) I . . . I don't want to watch any more.

GRACE. (*A real fight fan, she reports from the window.*) God, I love a good fight. C'mon, Will—c'mon, Will—give him the old uppercut. That'll do it every time. Oh, oh, what'd I tell you, the cowboy's down. Will's puttin' handcuffs on him now. (*Cherie sobs softly. Elma goes to her.*)

ELMA. Will'll give him first aid. He always does.

CHERIE. Well . . . you gotta admit. He had it comin'.

GRACE. (*Leaving the window now.*) I'm glad they got it settled outside. (*Looks around to see if anything needs to be straightened up.*) Remember the last time there was a fight in here, I had to put in a new window. (*She goes out rear door, and we become aware once more of Dr. Lyman, who gets up from the bench and weaves his way* C.)

DR. LYMAN. It takes strong men and women to love . . . (*About to fall, he grabs the back of a chair for support.*) People strong enough inside themselves to love . . . without humiliation. (*He sighs heavily and looks about him with blurred eyes.*) People big enough to grow with their love and live inside a whole, wide new dimension. People brave enough to bear the responsibility of *being* loved and not fear it as a burden. (*He sighs again and looks about him wearily.*) I . . . I never had the generosity to love, to give my own most private self to another, for I was *weak*. I thought the gift would somehow lessen *me. Me!* (*He laughs wildly and starts for the rear door.*) Romeo! Romeo! I am disgusting! (*Elma hurries after him, stopping him at the door.*)

ELMA. Dr. Lyman! Dr. Lyman!

DR. LYMAN. Don't bother, dear girl. Don't ever bother with a foolish old man like me.

ELMA. You're not a foolish old man. I like you more than anyone I've ever known.

49

DR. LYMAN. I'm flattered, my dear, and pleased, but you're young. In a few years, you will turn . . . from a girl into a woman; a kind, thoughtful, loving, intelligent woman . . . who could only pity me. For I'm a child, a drunken, unruly child, and I've nothing in my heart for a true woman. (*Grace returns through rear door in time to observe the rest of the scene. She is dressed now.*)

ELMA. Let me get you something to make you feel better.

DR. LYMAN. No . . . no . . . I shall seek the icy comfort of the rest room (*He rushes out the rear door. Cherie gets her robe, puts it on.*)

GRACE. (*Feeling concern for Elma.*) Elma, honey, what's the matter? What was he sayin' to you, Elma? (*Goes to her and they have a quiet talk between themselves as the action continues. Grace is quite motherly at these times. Now Virgil comes hurrying through the front door, going to Cherie.*)

VIRGIL. Miss, would ya help us? The sheriff says if you don't hold charges against Bo, he'll let him out to get back on the bus, if it ever goes.

CHERIE. So he can come back here and start maulin' me again? (*Grace pours glass of water, gives it to Elma.*)

VIRGIL. He won't do that no more, Miss. I promise.

CHERIE. *You promise!* How 'bout him?

VIRGIL. I think you can trust him now.

CHERIE. Thass what I thought before. Nothin' doin'. (*Starts L.*) He grabs ahold of a woman and kisses her . . . like he was Napoleon.

VIRGIL. (*Coming very close to speak as intimately as possible.*) Miss . . . if he was to know I told ya this, he'd never forgive me, but . . . yor the first woman he ever made love to at all.

CHERIE. Hah! I sure don't b'lieve that.

VIRGIL. It's true, Miss. He's allus been as shy as a rabbit.

CHERIE. (*In simple amazement.*) My God! (*Sits on chair at table.*)

GRACE. (*To Elma.*) Just take my advice and don't meet him in Topeka or anywhere else.

ELMA. I won't, Grace, but honest! I don't think he meant any harm. He just drinks a little too much. (*Dr. Lyman returns now through the rear door. Elma hurries to him.*) Dr. Lyman, are you all right?

50

DR. LYMAN. (*On his way to the bench.*) I'm an old man, my dear. I feel very weary. (*He stretches out on the bench, lying on his stomach. He goes almost immediately to sleep. Elma finds an old jacket and spreads it over his shoulders like a blanket. There is a long silence. Elma sits by Dr. Lyman attentively. Cherie is very preoccupied.*)

GRACE. Let him sleep it off. It's all you can do. (*Now Carl comes* 2.19A *in the rear door. There is a look of impatient disgust on his face, as though he had just witnessed some revolting insult. He casts a suspicious look at Dr. Lyman, now oblivious to everything, and turns to Grace.*)

CARL. Grace, fer Christ sake! who puked all over the backhouse?

GRACE. Oh, God! (*Dr. Lyman snores serenely.*) 2.20

CHERIE. (*Jumps up suddenly and grabs Virgil's jacket off hook.*) Come on, Virge. Let's go.

VIRGIL. (*Enthused.*) I'm awful glad you're gonna help him, Miss.

CHERIE. But if you're tellin' me a fib just to get him out of jail, I'll never forgive ya.

VIRGIL. It's no fib, Miss. You're the first gal he ever made love to at all.

CHERIE. Well, I sure ain't never had that honor before. (*They hurry out front door together.*)

CURTAIN

ACT III

By this time, it is early morning, about five o'clock. The storm has cleared, and outside the window we see the slow dawning, creeping above the distant hills, revealing a landscape all in peaceful white.

Bo, Cherie and Virgil are back now from the sheriff's office. Bo has returned to his corner, where he sits as before, with his back to the others, his head low. We can detect, if we study him, that one eye is blackened and one of his hands is bandaged. Virgil sits close to him on arm of bench, like an attendant. Dr. Lyman is still asleep on the bench, snoring loudly. Cherie tries to sleep at one of the tables. Elma is clearing the tables and sweeping. The only animated people right now are Carl and Grace. Carl is at the telephone trying to get the operator, and Grace is behind the counter.

CARL. (*After jiggling the receiver.*) Still dead. (*He bangs up.*)

GRACE. (*Yawns.*) I'll be glad when you all get out and I can go to bed. I'm tired.

CARL. (*Returning to counter, he sounds a trifle insinuating.*) Had enough a me, baby? (*Grace gives him a look, warning him not to let Elma overhear.*) I'm kinda glad the highway was blocked tonight.

GRACE. (*Coquettishly.*) Y'are?

CARL. Gave us a chance to become kinda acquainted, din it?

GRACE. Kinda!

CARL. Just pullin' in here three times a week, then pullin' out again in twenty minutes, I . . . I allus left . . . just wonderin' what you was like, Grace.

GRACE. I always wondered about *you*, too, Carl!

CARL. Ya did?

GRACE. Yah. But ya needn't go blabbing anything to the other drivers. (*Elma sweeps* U. S. *and toward front door* R.)

CARL. (*His honor offended.*) Why, what makes ya think I'd . . . ?

52

GRACE. Shoot! I know how you men talk when ya get t'gether. Worse'n women.

CARL. Well, not *me*, Grace.

GRACE. I certainly don't want the other drivers on this route, some of 'em especially, gettin' the idea I'm gonna serve 'em any more'n what they order over the counter.

CARL. Sure. I get ya. (*It occurs to him to feel flattered.*) But ya . . . ya kinda *liked* me . . . din ya, Grace?

GRACE (*Coquettish again.*) Maybe I did.

CARL. (*Trying to get more of a commitment out of her.*) Yah? Yah?

GRACE. Know what I first liked about ya, Carl? It was your hands. (*She takes one of his hands and plays with it.*) I like a man with big hands.

CARL. You got everything, baby. (*For just a moment, one senses the animal heat in their fleeting attraction.*) *Now Will comes stalking in through the front door, a man who is completely relaxed with the authority he possesses. He speaks to Grace.*)

WILL. (*Crosses L. to R. of Carl.*) One of the highway trucks just stopped by. They say it won't be very long now. (*Elma crosses D. R. to sweep near Cherie.*)

GRACE. I hope so.

WILL. (*With a look around.*) Everything peaceful?

GRACE. Yes, Will.

WILL. (*He studies Bo for a moment, then goes to him.*) Cowboy, if yor holdin' any grudges against me, I think ya oughta ask yourself what you'd'a done in my place. I couldn't let ya carry off the li'l lady when she din wanta go, could I? (*Bo has no answer. He just avoids Will's eyes. But Will is determined to get an answer.*) Could I? (*Grace leans on counter.*)

BO. I don't feel like talkin', Mister.

WILL. Well, I couldn't. And I think you might also remember that this li'l lady . . . (*Cherie begins to stir.*) if she wanted to . . . could press charges and get you sent to the penitentiary for violation of the Mann Act.

BO. The *what* act?

WILL. The Mann Act. You took a woman over the state line against her will.

VIRGIL. That'd be a serious charge, Bo.

53

BO. (*Stands facing Will.*) I loved her. (*Virgil crosses* D. R. *near door.*)

WILL. That don't make any difference.

BO. A man's gotta right to the things he loves.

WILL. Not unless he deserves 'em, cowboy.

BO. I'm a hard-workin' man, I own me my own ranch, I got six thousand dollars in the bank.

WILL. A man don't deserve the things he loves, unless he kin be a little humble about gettin' 'em.

BO. (*Comes* D. R., *sits at chair* R. *of* C. *table.*) I ain't gonna get down on my knees and beg. (*Virgil crosses* D. S. L. *of* R. *table.*)

WILL. Bein' humble ain't the same thing as bein' *wretched*. (*Bo doesn't understand.*) I had to learn that once, too, cowboy. I wasn't quite as old as you. I stole horses instead of women because you could *sell* horses. One day, I stole a horse off the wrong man, the Rev. Hezekiah Pearson. I never thought I'd get mine from any preacher, but he was very fair. Gave me every chance to put myself clear. But I wouldn't admit the horse was his. Finally, he did what he had to do. He threshed me to within a inch of my life. I never forgot. 'Cause it was the first time in my life, I had to admit I was wrong. I was miserable. Finally, after a few days, I decided the only thing to do was to admit to the man how I felt. Then I felt different about the whole thing. I joined his church, and we was bosom pals till he died a few years ago. (*He turns to Virgil.*) Has he done what I asked him to?

VIRGIL. Not yet, sheriff. (*Sits at a table.*)

WILL. (*To Bo.*) Why should ya be so scared?

BO. Who says I'm scared?

WILL. Ya gimme yor word, didn't ya?

BO. (*Somewhat resentful.*) I'm gonna do it, if ya'll jest gimme time.

WILL. But I warn ya, it ain't gonna do no good unless you really mean it. (*Elma is* R. *with dust pan.*)

BO. I'll mean it.

WILL. All right then. Go ahead. (*Will crosses* U. C. *Slowly, reluctantly, Bo gets to his feet and awkwardly, like a guilty boy, makes his way over to the counter to Grace. Carl crosses to stove.*)

BO. Miss, I . . . I wanna apologize.

GRACE. What for?

BO. Fer causin' such a commotion.

GRACE. Ya needn't apologize to *me*, cowboy. I like a good fight. You're welcome at Grace's Diner *any* time. I mean *any* time.

BO. (*With an appreciative grin.*) Thanks. (*Now he goes to Elma* u. R.) I musta acted like a hoodlum. I apologize.

ELMA. (*Steps* L. *to him.*) Oh, that's all right.

BO. Thank ya, Miss.

ELMA. (*Crosses* L., *empties dust pan in can under sink.*) I'm awfully sorry we never got to see your rope tricks. (*Puts broom and dust pan away, sits on stool.*)

BO. They ain't much. (*Pointing to the sleeping Dr. Lyman.*) Have I gotta wake up the perfessor t'apologize t'him? (*Carl drifts toward counter.*)

WILL. You can overlook the perfessor. (*He nods toward Cherie, whom Bo dreads to confront, most of all. He starts toward her but doesn't get very far.*)

BO. I cain't do it. (*Turns* u. c. *Virgil rises.*)

VIRGIL. (*Disappointed.*) Aw, Bo!

BO. I jest cain't do it.

WILL. (*Crosses* D. L. *a few steps.*) Why not?

BO. She'd have no respeck for me now. She saw me beat.

WILL. (*Crosses to him.*) You gave me your promise. You owe that girl an apology, whether you got beat or not, and you're going to say it to her or I'm not lettin' you back on the bus. (*Bo is in a dilemma. He wipes his brow.*)

VIRGIL. G'wan, Bo. G'wan. (*Steps* u. L.)

BO. Well . . . I . . . I'll try. (*He makes his way to her tortuously and finally gets out her name.*) Cherry!

CHERIE. (*Rises*) Yah?

BO. Cherry . . . it wasn't right a me to treat ya the way I did, draggin' ya onto the bus, tryin' to make ya marry me whether ya wanted to or not. Ya think ya could ever forgive me?

CHERIE. (*After some consideration*) I guess I been treated worse in my life.

BO. (*Taking out his wallet.*) Cherry . . . I got ya here and I think I oughta get ya back in good style. So . . . take this. (*He hands her a bill.*)

CHERIE. Did the sheriff make you do this?

BO. (*Angrily.*) No, by God! He din say nothin' 'bout my givin' ya money.

WILL. (*Crosses* D. L. *of Cherie's table.*) That's his idea, Miss. But I think it's a good one.

CHERIE. Ya don't have to gimme this much, Bo.

BO. I want ya to have it.

CHERIE. Thanks. I can sure use it.

BO. And I . . . I wish ya good luck, Cherry . . . Honest I do.

CHERIE. I wish you the same, Bo.

BO. Well . . . I guess I said ev'rything that's to be said, so . . . so long.

CHERIE. (*In a tiny voice.*) So long. (*Awkward and embarrassed now, Bo returns to his corner, and Cherie sits back down at the table, full of wistful wonder.*)

WILL. Now that wasn't so bad, was it, son?

BO. I'd ruther break in wild horses than have to do it again. (*Will laughs heartily, then strolls over to the counter in a seemingly casual way.*)

WILL. How's your headache, Grace?

GRACE. Huh?

WILL. A while back, you said you had a headache.

GRACE. Oh, I feel fine now, Will.

WILL. (*He looks at Carl.*) You have a nice walk, Carl?

CARL. Yah. Sure.

WILL. Well, I think ya better go upstairs 'cause someone took your overshoes and left 'em outside the door to Grace's apartment. (*Will laughs long and heartily, and Elma cannot suppress a grin. Carl looks at his feet and realizes his oversight. Grace is indignant.*)

GRACE. Nosy old snoop!

WILL. I'll have me a cup of coffee, Grace, and one a these sweet rolls. (*He selects a roll from the glass dish on counter, sits on a stool. Grace motions Elma to get Will coffee, which she does.*)

VIRGIL. Come on over to the counter now, Bo, and have a bite a breakfast.

BO. I ain't hungry, Virge.

VIRGIL. Maybe a cup a coffee? (*Grace sits on stool behind counter.*)

BO. I couldn't get it down.

VIRGIL. Now what's the matter, Bo? Ya oughta feel purty good. The sheriff let ya go and . . .

BO. I might as well a stayed in the jail.

VIRGIL. Now, what kinda talk is that? The bus'll be leavin' purty soon and we'll be back at the ranch in a coupla days.

BO. I don't care if I never see that dang ranch again.

VIRGIL. Why, Bo, you worked half yor life earnin' the money to build it up.

BO. It's the lonesomest damn place I ever did see.

VIRGIL. Well . . . I never thought so.

BO. It'll be like goin' back to a graveyard.

VIRGIL. Bo . . . I heard Hank and Orville talkin' 'bout the new school marm, lives over to the Stebbins'. They say she's a looker.

BO. I ain't int'rested in no school marm.

VIRGIL. Give yourself time, Bo. Yor young. You'll find lotsa gals, gals that'll love *you*, too.

BO. I want Cherry. (*And for the first time we observe he is capable of tears.*)

VIRGIL. (*With a futile shrug of his shoulders.*) Aw—Bo ——

BO. (*Dismissing him.*) Go git yorself somethin' t'eat, Virge. (*Bo remains in isolated gloom as Virgil makes his slow way to the counter. Suddenly the telephone rings. Grace jumps to answer it. Elma gives Virgil coffee. He sits on stool to drink it.*)

GRACE. My God! the lines are up. (*Into the telephone.*) Grace's Diner! (*Pause.*) It is? (*Pause.*) O.K. I'll tell him. (*Hangs up and turns to Carl.*) Road's cleared now but you're gonna have to put on your chains 'cause the road's awful slick.

CARL. God damn! (*Gets up and bustles into his overcoat, going c. to make his announcement.*) Road's clear, folks! Bus'll be ready to leave as soon as I get the chains on. That'll take about twenty minutes . . . (*Stops and looks back at them.*) . . . unless someone wants to help me. (*Goes out front door. Will gets up from the counter*)

WILL. I'll help ya, Carl. (*He goes out front door. Cherie makes her way over to Bo.*)

CHERIE. Bo?

BO. Yah?

CHERIE. I just wanted to tell ya somethin', Bo. It's kinda personal and kinda embarrassin', too, but . . . I ain't the kinda gal you thought I was. (*Elma and Grace are busy clearing counter.*)

BO. What ya mean, Cherry?

CHERIE. Well, I guess some people'd say I led a real wicked life. I guess I have.

57

BO. What ya tryin' to tell me?

CHERIE. Well . . . I figgered since ya found me at the Blue Dragon, ya just took it fer granted I'd had other boy friends 'fore you.

BO. Ya had?

CHERIE. Yes, Bo. Quite a few.

BO. Virge'd told me that, but I wouldn't b'lieve him.

CHERIE. Well, it's true. So ya see . . . I ain't the kinda gal ya want at all. (*Bo is noncommittal. Cherie slips back to her table. Elma makes her way to the bench to rouse Dr. Lyman.*)

ELMA. Dr. Lyman! Dr. Lyman! (*He comes to with a jump, staring out wildly about him.*)

DR. LYMAN. Where am I? (*Recognizing Elma.*) Oh, it's you. (*A great smile appears. Rises.*) Dear girl. What a sweet awakening!

ELMA. How do you feel?

DR. LYMAN. That's not a polite question. How long have I been asleep here?

ELMA. Oh—a couple of hours. (*Grace sits on stool.*)

DR. LYMAN. Sometimes Nature blesses me with a total blackout. I seem to remember absolutely nothing after we started our performance. How were we?

ELMA. Marvelous.

DR. LYMAN. Oh, I'm glad. Now I'll have a cup of that coffee you were trying to force on me last night.

ELMA. All right. (*Crosses to u. s. end of counter.*) Can I fix you something to eat?

DR. LYMAN. No. Nothing to eat. (*He makes a face of repugnance.*)

ELMA. Oh, Dr. Lyman, you *must* eat something. Really.

DR. LYMAN. *Must* I?

ELMA. Oh, yes! Please!

DR. LYMAN. Very well, for your sweet sake, I'll have a couple of three-minute eggs, and some toast and orange juice. But I'm doing this for you, mind you. Just for you. (*Elma slips behind the counter to begin his breakfast, as Virgil gets up from the counter and goes to Bo. Dr. Lyman slowly crosses to counter and sits on stool.*)

VIRGIL. I'll go help the driver with his chains, Bo. You stay here

58

and take care a that hand. (*He goes out front door. Bo finds his way again to Cherie. Grace is working behind counter with Elma.*)

BO. Cherry . . . would I be molestin' ya if I said somethin'?

CHERIE. (*Rises as Bo crosses to her.*) No . . .

BO. Well . . . since you brought the subject up, you *are* the first gal I ever had anything to do with. (*There is a silence.*) By God! I never thought I'd hear m'self sayin' that, but I said it.

CHERIE. I never woulda guessed it, Bo.

BO. Ya see . . . I'd lived all my life on a ranch . . . and I guess I din know much about women . . . 'cause they're *diff'rent* from men.

CHERIE. Well, natur'ly.

BO. Every time I got around one . . . I began to feel kinda scared . . . and I din know how t'act. It was aggravatin'.

CHERIE. Ya wasn't scared with *me*, Bo.

BO. When I come into that night club place, you was singin' . . . and you smiled at me while you was singin', and winked at me a coupla times. Remember?

CHERIE. Yah. I remember.

BO. Well, I guess I'm kinda green, but . . . no gal ever done that to me before, so I thought you was singin' yor songs just fer *me*.

CHERIE. Ya did kinda attrack me, Bo . . .

BO. Anyway, you was so purty, and ya seemed so kinda warm-hearted and sweet. I . . . I felt like I *could* love ya . . . and I did.

CHERIE. Bo—ya think you really did love me?

BO. Why, Cherry! I couldn't be *familiar* . . . with a gal I din love. (*Cherie is brought almost to tears. Neither she nor Bo can find any more words for the moment, and drift away from each other back to their respective places. At the counter Dr. Lyman*³·¹¹ *eats his breakfast, which Elma has served him. Carl comes back in front door, followed by Virgil and Will. Carl has got his overshoes on now. He comes C. again to make an announcement.*)

CARL. Bus headed west! All aboard! Next stop, Topeka! (*He rejoins Grace at the counter and, taking a pencil from his pocket, begins making out his report. Will speaks to Bo.*) ³·¹²

WILL. How ya feelin' now, cowboy?

BO. I ain't the happiest critter that was ever born.

WILL. Just 'cause ya ain't happy now don't mean ya ain't gonna be happy t'morrow. Feel like shakin' hands now, cowboy?

BO. (*Hesitant.*) Well . . .

VIRGIL. Go on, Bo. He's only trying to be friends.

BO. (*Offering his hand, still somewhat reluctantly.*) I don't mind. (*They shake.*)

WILL. I just want you to remember there's no hard feelin's. So long.

BO. S'long.

WILL. I'm goin' home now, Grace. See you Monday.

GRACE. S'long, Will.

CARL. Thanks for helpin' me, Will. I'll be pullin' out, soon as I make out the reports.

WILL. (*Stops at the door and gives a final word to Cherie.*) Montana's not a bad place, Miss. (*He goes out front door.*)

VIRGIL. Nice fella, Bo.

BO. (*Concentrating on Cherie.*) Maybe I'll think so some day.

VIRGIL. Well, maybe we better be boardin' the bus, Bo. (*Without even hearing Virgil, Bo makes his way suddenly over to Cherie.*)

BO. Cherry!

CHERIE. Hi, Bo!

BO. Cherry, I promised not to molest ya, but if you was to give yor permission, it'd be all right. I . . . I'd like to kiss ya g'by.

CHERIE. Ya would? (*Bo nods.*) I'd like ya to kiss me, Bo. I really would. (*A wide grin cracks open his face and he becomes all hoodlum boy again, about to take her in his arms roughly as he did before, but she stops him.*) Bo! I think this time when ya kiss me, it oughta be diff'rent.

BO. (*Not sure what she means.*) Oh! (*He looks around at Virgil who turns quickly away, as though admitting his inability to advise his buddy. Bo then takes her in his arms cautiously, as though holding a precious object that was still a little strange to him.*)

BO. Golly! When ya kiss someone fer serious, it's kinda scarey, ain't it?

CHERIE. Yah! It is. (*Anyway, he kisses her, long and tenderly.*)

GRACE. (*At the counter.*) It don't look like he was molestin' her now. (*Bo, after the kiss is ended, is dazed. Uncertain of his feelings, he stampedes across the room to Virgil, drawing him to the*

*bench where the two men can confer. The action continues with
Dr. Lyman, at the counter, having his breakfast.)*

DR. LYMAN. I could tell you with all honesty that this was the
most delicious breakfast I've ever eaten, but it wouldn't be much
of a compliment because I have eaten very few breakfasts. *(They
laugh together.)*

ELMA. It's my favorite meal. *(Turns to the refrigerator as he
brings bottle out secretly and spikes his coffee.)*

DR. LYMAN. *(When Elma returns.)* Dear girl, let us give up our
little spree, shall we? You don't want to go. traipsing over the
streets of the State's capital with an old reprobate like me.

ELMA. Whatever you say.

DR. LYMAN. I shall continue my way to Denver. I'm sure it's
best.

ELMA. Anyway, I've certainly enjoyed knowing you.

DR. LYMAN. Thank you. Ah! sometimes it is so gratifying to
feel that one is doing the "right" thing, I wonder that I don't
choose to always.

ELMA. What do you mean?

DR. LYMAN. Oh, I was just rambling. You know, perhaps while
I am in the vicinity of Topeka, I should drop in at that hospital
and seek some advice.

ELMA. Sometimes their patients come in here. They look perfectly
all right to me.

DR. LYMAN. Friends have been hinting for quite a while that I
should get psychoanalyzed. *(He chuckles.)* I don't know if they
had my best interests at heart or their own.

ELMA. Golly. I don't see anything the matter with you.

DR. LYMAN. *(A little sadly.)* No. Young people never do. *(Now
with a return of high spirits.)* However, I don't think I care to be
psychoanalyzed. I rather cherish myself as I am. *(The cavalier
again, he takes her hand.)* Good-bye, my dear! You were the
loveliest Juliet since Miss Jane Cowl. *(Kisses her hand gallantly,
then goes for his coat. Elma comes from behind counter and follows him.)*

ELMA. Thank you, Dr. Lyman. I feel it's been an honor to know
you. You're the smartest man I've ever met.

DR. LYMAN. The smartest?

ELMA. Really you are.

DR. LYMAN. Oh, yes. I'm terribly smart. Wouldn't it have been nice . . . to be intelligent? (*He chuckles, blows a kiss to her, then hurries out the front door. Elma lingers behind, watching him get on the bus.*)

3.15

CARL. (*To Grace.*) Hey, know what I heard about the perfessor? The detective at the bus terminal in Kanz City is a buddy a mine. He pointed out the perfessor to me before he got on the bus. Know what he said? He said the p'lice in Kanz City picked the perfessor up for *loiterin'* round the schools.

GRACE. (*Appalled.*) Honest?

CARL. Then they checked his record and found he'd been in trouble several times, for gettin' involved with young girls.

GRACE. My God! Did you tell Will?

CARL. Sure, I told him. They ain't *got* anything on the perfessor now, so there's nothin' Will could do. (*Elma makes her way back to the counter now and hears the rest of what Carl has to say.*) What gets *me* is why does he call hisself a doctor? Is he some kinda phony?

ELMA. (*Going behind counter.*) No, Carl. He's a Doctor of Philosophy.

CARL. What's that?

ELMA. It's the very highest degree there is, for scholarship.

GRACE. Ya'd think he'd have philosophy enough to keep outa trouble. (*Elma resumes her work behind the counter now.*)

3.15a

CARL. (*To Grace.*) Sorry to see me go, baby?

GRACE. No . . . I told ya, I'm tired.

CARL. (*Good-naturedly.*) Ya know, sometimes I get to thinkin', what the hell good is marriage, where ya have to put up with the same broad every day, and lookit her in the morning, and try to get along with her when she's got a bad disposition. This way suits me fine.

GRACE. I got no complaints, either. Incidentally, are you married, Carl?

CARL. Now, who said I was married, Grace? Who said it? You just tell me and I'll fix him.

GRACE. Relax! Relax! See ya day after tomorrow. (*She winks at him.*)

CARL. (*Winks back.*) You might get surprised . . . what can happen in twenty minutes. (*Slaps Grace on the buttocks as a gesture of farewell.*) All aboard! (*He bustles out the front door as Bo hurries to Cherie. Elma and Grace work behind counter.*)

GRACE. (*To herself.*) He still never said whether he was married. 3.16

BO. Cherry?

CHERIE. (*A little expectantly.*) Yah?

BO. I been talkin' with my buddy, and he thinks I'm virgin enough fer the two of us.

CHERIE. (*Snickers, very amused.*) Honest? Did Virgil say that?

BO. Yah . . . and I like ya like ya are, Cherry. So I don't care how ya got that way.

CHERIE. (*Deeply touched.*) Oh, God, thass the sweetest, tenderest thing that was ever said to me.

BO. (*Feeling awkward.*) Cherry . . . it's awful hard for a fella, after he's been turned down once, to git up enough guts to try again . . .

CHERIE. Ya don't need guts, Bo.

BO. (*Not quite sure what she means.*) I don't?

CHERIE. It's the last thing in the world ya need.

BO. Well . . . anyway, I jest don't have none now, so I'll . . . just have to say what I feel in my heart.

CHERIE. Yah?

BO. I still wish you was goin' back to the ranch with me, more'n anything I know.

CHERIE. Ya do?

BO. Yah. I do.

CHERIE. Why, I'd go anywhere in the world with ya now, Bo. Anywhere at all.

BO. Ya would? Ya would? (*They have a fast embrace. All look.*)

GRACE. (*Nudging Elma.*) I knew this was gonna happen all the time.

ELMA. Gee, I didn't. (*Now Bo and Cherie break apart, both running to opposite sides of the room. Bo to tell Virgil, Cherie, Elma. Virgil rises.*)

BO. Hear that, Virge? Yahoo! We're gettin' married after all. Cherry's goin' back with me.

CHERIE. (*At counter.*) Ain't it wonderful when someone so awful turns out t'be so nice? We're gettin' married. I'm goin' to Montana. (*Carl sticks his head through the door and calls impatiently. Cherie gets suitcase from behind counter, and jacket.*) 3.17

CARL. Hey! All aboard, fer Christ's sake! (*He goes out front door. Bo grabs Virgil now by the arm. Cherie goes to him, puts suitcase down.*)

63

BO. C'mon, Virge, y'old raccoon!

VIRGIL. (*Demurring.*) Now look, Bo . . . listen t'me for a second.

BO. (*Who can't listen to anything in his high revelry. One arm is around Cherie, the other tugs at Virgil.*) C'mon! Doggone it, we wasted enough time. Let's git goin'.

VIRGIL. (*Pulls away.*) Listen, Bo. Now be quiet jest a minute. You gotta hear me, Bo. You don't need me no more. I ain't goin'.

BO. (*Not believing his ears.*) You ain't *what?*

VIRGIL. I . . . I ain't goin' with ya, Bo.

BO. (*Flabbergasted.*) Well, what ya know about that?

VIRGIL. It's best I don't, Bo.

BO. Jest one blame catastrophe after another.

VIRGIL. I . . . I got another job in mind, Bo. Where the feed's mighty good, and I'll be lookin' after the cattle. I meant to tell ya 'bout it 'fore this.

BO. Virge, I can't b'lieve you'd leave yor old sidekick. Yor jokin', man.

VIRGIL. No . . . I ain't jokin', Bo. I ain't.

BO. Well, I'll be a . . .

CHERIE. Virgil—I wish you'd come. I liked *you* . . . 'fore I ever liked Bo.

BO. Ya *know* Cherry likes ya, Virge. It jest don't make sense, yor not comin'.

VIRGIL. Well . . . I'm doin' the right thing. I know I am.

BO. Who's gonna look after the cattle?

VIRGIL. Hank. Every bit as good as *I* ever was.

BO. (*Very disheartened.*) Aw, Virge, I dunno why ya have to pull a stunt like this.

VIRGIL. You better hurry, Bo. That driver's not gonna wait all day.

BO. (*Starting to pull Virgil, to drag him away just as he tried once with Cherie.*) Daggone it, yor my buddy, and I ain't gonna let ya go. Yor goin' *with* Cherry and me 'cause we want ya . . .

VIRGIL. (*It's getting very hard for him to control his feelings.*) No . . . No . . . lemme be, Bo . . .

CHERIE. (*Holding Bo back.*) Bo . . . ya can't do it that way . . . ya jest can't . . . if he don't wanta go, ya can't make him . . .

BO. But, Cherry, there ain't a reason in the world he shouldn't go. It's plumb crazy.

CHERIE. Well, sometimes people have their *own* reasons, Bo.

BO. Oh? (*He reconsiders.*) Well, I just hate to think of gettin' along without old Virge.

VIRGIL. (*Laughing.*) In a couple weeks . . . ya'll never miss me.

BO. (*Disheartened.*) Aw, Virge!

VIRGIL Get along with ya now.

CHERIE. Virgil—(*Brightly.*) will ya come and visit us, Virgil?

VIRGIL. I'll be up in the summer.

BO. Where ya gonna be, Virge?

VIRGIL. I'll write ya th' address. Don't have time to give it to ya now. Nice place. Mighty nice. Now hurry and get on your bus. (*Carl bonks the horn off* R.)

BO. (*Managing a quick embrace.*) So long, old boy. So long!

VIRGIL. 'Bye, Bo! G'bye! (*Now, to stave off any tears, Bo grabs Cherie's hand.*)

BO. C'mon, Cherry. Let's make it fast. (*Before they are out the door, a thought occurs to Bo. He stops, takes off his leather jacket and helps Cherie into it. He has been gallant. Then he picks up her suitcase and they go out the front door, calling their farewells behind them.*)

CHERIE. 'Bye—'bye—'bye, everyone! 'Bye! (*Virgil stands at the door, waving good-bye. Elma runs to window. His eyes look a little moist. In a moment, the bus's motor is heard to start up. Then the bus leaves.*)   3.18

GRACE. (*From behind counter.*) Mister, we gotta close this place up now, if Elma and me're gonna get any rest. We won't be open again till eight o'clock when the day girl comes on. The next bus through is to Albuquerque, at eight forty-five. (*Elma returns to counter.*)

VIRGIL. Albuquerque? I guess that's as good a place as any. (*He remains by the front entrance, looking out on the frosty morning.* 3.19 *Elma and Grace continue their work behind the counter.*)

ELMA. Poor Dr. Lyman!

CRACE. Say, did you hear what Carl told me about that guy?

ELMA. No. What was it, Grace?

GRACE. Well, according to Carl, they run him outa Kanz City.

ELMA. I don't believe it.

GRACE. Honey, Carl got it straight from the detective at the bus terminal.

ELMA. (*Afraid to ask.*) What . . . did Dr. Lyman do?

GRACE. Well, lots of old fogies like him just can't let young girls alone. (*A wondering look comes over Elma's face.*) So, it's a good thing you didn't meet him in Topeka.

ELMA. Do you think . . . he wanted to make *love*, to *me*?

GRACE. I don't think he meant to play hopscotch.

ELMA. (*Very moved.*) Gee!

GRACE. Next time any guy comes in here and starts gettin' fresh, you come tell your Aunt Grace. (*Virgil is seated on chair by a table.*)

ELMA. I guess I'm kinda stupid.

GRACE. (*Elma is at* c.) Everyone has gotta learn. (*Looking into refrigerator.*) Now Monday, for sure, I gotta order some cheese.

ELMA. I'll remind you.

GRACE. (*Coming to Elma, apologetically.*) Elma, honey?

ELMA. Yes?

GRACE. I could kill Will Masters for sayin' anything about me and Carl. I didn't want you to know.

ELMA. I don't see why I shouldn't know, Grace. I don't wanta be a baby forever.

GRACE. Of course you don't. But still, you're a kid, and I don't wanta set no examples or anything. Do you think you can overlook it and not think bad of me?

ELMA. Sure, Grace.

GRACE. 'Cause I'm a restless sort of woman, and every once in a while, I gotta have me a man, just to keep m'self from gettin' grouchy. (*Elma goes behind counter.*)

ELMA. It's not my business, Grace. (*She stops a moment to consider herself in the mirror, rather pleased.*) Just think, he wanted to make love to *me*.

GRACE. Now don't start gettin' stuck on yourself.

ELMA. I'm not, Grace. But it's nice to know that someone *can* feel that way.

GRACE. You're not gonna have any trouble. Just wait'll you get to college and start meeting all those cute *boys*. (*Grace seems to savor this.*)

ELMA. All right. I'll wait.

GRACE. (*Takes apron off.*) You can run along now, honey. All I gotta do is empty the garbage.

ELMA. (*Getting her coat from closet behind counter.*) O.K.

GRACE. G'night!

ELMA. (*Coming from behind counter, slipping into her coat.*) Good night, Grace. See you Monday. (*Passing Virgil.*) It was very nice knowing you, Virgil, and I just loved your music.

VIRGIL. Thank you, Miss. G'night. (*Elma goes out front door.*)

GRACE. We're closing now, Mister.

VIRGIL. (*Coming* C.) Any place warm I could stay till eight o'clock?

GRACE. Now that the p'lice station's closed, I don't know where you could go, unless ya wanted to take a chance of wakin' up the man that runs the hotel.

VIRGIL. No—I wouldn't wanta be any trouble.

GRACE. There'll be a bus to Kanz City in a few minutes. I'll put the sign out and they'll stop.

VIRGIL. No, thanks. No point a goin' back there.

GRACE. Then I'm sorry, Mister, but you're just left out in the cold. (*She carries a can of garbage out the rear door leaving Virgil for the moment alone.*)

VIRGIL. (*To himself.*) Well . . . that's what happens to some people. (*Quietly, he picks up his guitar and goes out. Grace comes back in, locks back door, snaps wall switch, then yawns and stretches, then sees that the front door is locked. The sun outside is just high enough now to bring a dim light into the restaurant. Grace stops at the rear door and casts her eyes tiredly over the establishment. One senses her aloneness. She sighs, then goes out the door. A cold sweep of morning wind whistles over the countryside. The curtain comes down on an empty stage.*)

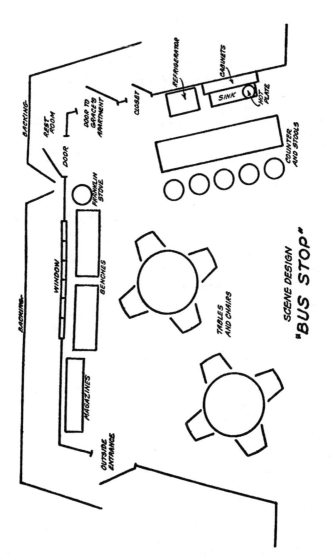

SCENE DESIGN
"BUS STOP"

REFRIGERATOR

CABINETS

SINK

HOT PLATE

COUNTER AND STOOLS

CLOSET

DOOR TO GRACE'S APARTMENT

REST ROOM

BACKING

DOOR

FRANKLIN STOVE

WINDOW

BENCHES

TABLES AND CHAIRS

BACKING

MAGAZINES

OUTSIDE ENTRANCE

PROP CHECK SHEET

Elma and Grace's coats in closet (Grace's scarf and Elma's cap)
Newspaper (2 parts) and magazine on R. end of bench
Shakespeare book—C. of rack
Wicker chair—6 inches from R. wall
D. R. chair—horizontally level
Spittoons—1 by mag rack, 1 D. R. corner
Broom and dustpan—D. S. of refrig. under sink
Ashtrays (with butts) each table
No. 4 stool—8 inches below counter
2 ashtrays—counter
Used plate, cup, silver, crumpled napkin, bread crusts, D. S. on counter
1 creamer with milk by urn
1 sugar D. S. on counter
2 sugars U. S. on counter
Keys in cash drawer
Money, paper and coins in cash drawer
Yellow pitcher with fresh water—shelf under cash drawer
2 tumbler glasses—U. S. end of shelf under curve of counter
3 juice glasses—under cash drawer
Elma's knitting—shelf under curve of counter
Garbage pail (lid off) U. S. of division under counter
Small stool—D. S. of division under counter
Garbage can (lid on) under urn
2 ashtrays on window sill
5 cups on shelf above urn
5 cups along side of urn
Glass with spoons by urn
Large plates on shelf
Sandwich plates on shelf
6 glasses on drain
4 sandwich plates on drain
Dish towels (2) on hook
Dish cloth in sink
Plate with hamburger buns (12 round cuts whole wheat bread) above
    griddle
Loaf whole wheat bread above griddle
Butcher knife, and butter knife above griddle

2 small skillets (one with fake fried eggs, upside down, D. s. on griddle
Pancake turner
Small sauce pan
Refrigerator
    Lemon soda
    Ham on plate—2 slices
    3 slices bolony on plate separated by wax paper
    Quart milk
    Marmalade jar
    6 hardboiled or fake eggs
    Orange juice in pitcher
Coffee in urn (six cups)
Mirror over sink
OFF-STAGE WATER TANK—FULL
Prop table
    OFF R.:
        Whiskey bottle—full—Dr. Lyman
        Book—Dr. Lyman
        Suitcase—Cherie
        Purse with cigarettes, money, etc.—Cherie
        Guitar in case—Virge
        Thermos jug—Will
        Bandage, adhesive tape, white bandaids—Bo
        Coins
        Playing cards—Virge

SET FOR ACT II

Stool behind counter
Movie mag to C. table
Fold paper on bench and strike to behind magazines
Donut and roll tray to top of refrigerator
Bottle and drink glass (Dr. Lyman's) C. of counter (by No. 2)
Clear counter except ashtrays (napkins, salt and pepper, sugar to
    shelf)
Strike sugars from tables
Book on counter—strike
Bo's jacket on bench—over back of bench
Suitcase behind counter (PACK WITH COSTUME AND ROBE)
Cherie's hat and jacket D. s. on counter
Switch small stool and garbage can under counter (stool u. s. of di-
    vision garbage can D. s.)
Virgil's coat on No. 4 hook in the clear. Hat on floor
Dr. Lyman's scarf to bench

SET FOR ACT III

Wicker chair
Chair R. of C. table—move out
Ashtray from counter to C. table
Donut and roll plate to counter (at curve)
Napkins and sugar to counter
Guitar in case D. R.
Apricot (2 halves) in cup hidden by stove
Load suitcase with weights, check clasps
Check Dr. Lyman's bottle—bench
Bo's hat D. R. D. S. hook
Cherie's jacket and hat to R. table
Dr. Lyman's scarf on hook with coat in the clear—No. 3 hook
Check Bo for bandages
Check Carl's coat and cap in closet
Sauce pan with water on top of griddle
FRESH COFFEE IN URN (4 cups)
Re-set stools
Pencil and paper for Carl

NEW PLAYS

★ **CLYBOURNE PARK by Bruce Norris.** WINNER OF THE 2011 PULITZER PRIZE AND 2012 TONY AWARD. Act One takes place in 1959 as community leaders try to stop the sale of a home to a black family. Act Two is set in the same house in the present day as the now predominantly African-American neighborhood battles to hold its ground. "Vital, sharp-witted and ferociously smart." –*NY Times.* "A theatrical treasure…Indisputably, uproariously funny." –*Entertainment Weekly.* [4M, 3W] ISBN: 978-0-8222-2697-0

★ **WATER BY THE SPOONFUL by Quiara Alegría Hudes.** WINNER OF THE 2012 PULITZER PRIZE. A Puerto Rican veteran is surrounded by the North Philadelphia demons he tried to escape in the service. "This is a very funny, warm, and yes uplifting play." –*Hartford Courant.* "The play is a combination poem, prayer and app on how to cope in an age of uncertainty, speed and chaos." –*Variety.* [4M, 3W] ISBN: 978-0-8222-2716-8

★ **RED by John Logan.** WINNER OF THE 2010 TONY AWARD. Mark Rothko has just landed the biggest commission in the history of modern art. But when his young assistant, Ken, gains the confidence to challenge him, Rothko faces the agonizing possibility that his crowning achievement could also become his undoing. "Intense and exciting." –*NY Times.* "Smart, eloquent entertainment." –*New Yorker.* [2M] ISBN: 978-0-8222-2483-9

★ **VENUS IN FUR by David Ives.** Thomas, a beleaguered playwright/director, is desperate to find an actress to play Vanda, the female lead in his adaptation of the classic sadomasochistic tale *Venus in Fur.* "Ninety minutes of good, kinky fun." –*NY Times.* "A fast-paced journey into one man's entrapment by a clever, vengeful female." –*Associated Press.* [1M, 1W] ISBN: 978-0-8222-2603-1

★ **OTHER DESERT CITIES by Jon Robin Baitz.** Brooke returns home to Palm Springs after a six-year absence and announces that she is about to publish a memoir dredging up a pivotal and tragic event in the family's history—a wound they don't want reopened. "Leaves you feeling both moved and gratifyingly sated." –*NY Times.* "A genuine pleasure." –*NY Post.* [2M, 3W] ISBN: 978-0-8222-2605-5

★ **TRIBES by Nina Raine.** Billy was born deaf into a hearing family and adapts brilliantly to his family's unconventional ways, but it's not until he meets Sylvia, a young woman on the brink of deafness, that he finally understands what it means to be understood. "A smart, lively play." –*NY Times.* "[A] bright and boldly provocative drama." –*Associated Press.* [3M, 2W] ISBN: 978-0-8222-2751-9

DRAMATISTS PLAY SERVICE, INC.
440 Park Avenue South, New York, NY 10016 212-683-8960 Fax 212-213-1539
postmaster@dramatists.com www.dramatists.com

BUS STOP
by William Inge

5M, 3W

In the middle of a howling snowstorm, a bus out of Kansas City pulls up a cheerful roadside diner. All roads are blocked, and four or five weary travelers are going to have to hole up until morning. Cherie, a nightclub chanteuse in a sparkling gown and a seedy fur-trimmed jacket, is the passenger with most to worry about. She's been pursued, made love to, and finally kidnapped by a twenty-one-year-old cowboy with a ranch of his own and the romantic methods of an unusually headstrong bull. The belligerent cowhand is right behind her, ready to sling her over his shoulder and carry her, alive and kicking, all the way to Montana. Even as she's ducking out from under his clumsy but confident embraces, and screeching at him fiercely to shut him up, she pauses to furrow her forehead and muse, "Somehow deep inside of me I got a funny feeling I'm gonna end up in Montana ..." As a counterpoint to the main romance, the proprietor of the cafe and the bus driver at last find time to develop a friendship of their own; a middle-age scholar comes to terms with himself; and a young girl who works in the cafe also gets her first taste of romance.

"... Mr. Inge has put together an uproarious comedy that never strays from the truth." —**The New York Times**

"William Inge should be a great comfort to all of us ... he brings to the theatre a kind of warm-hearted compassion, creative vigor, freshness of approach and appreciation of average humanity that can be wonderfully touching and stimulating." —**The New York P**

Also by William Inge
PICNIC
A LOSS OF ROSES
NATURAL AFFECTION
and many others

ISBN 978-0-8222-0166-3

DRAMATISTS PLAY SERVICE, INC.

9 780822 201663